Sharon McGovern was abused by her stepfather from the age of four to seventeen years of age. In a step of unprecedented bravery she finally confronted her abuser and saw justice done when he was charged and convicted of seven accounts of rape and indecent assault. Sharon continues her work with rape and abuse victims and speaks publicly on how to help survivors of crime. She lives in Grays, Essex with her family.

Afraid

Sharon McGovern

An Orion paperback

First published in Great Britain in 2008
by Orion
This paperback edition published in 2009
by Orion Books Ltd,
Orion House, 5 Upper St Martin's Lane,
London WC2H 9EA

An Hachette UK company

3 5 7 9 10 8 6 4 2

Copyright © Sharon McGovern 2009

A CIP catalogue record for this book is available
from the British Library.

ISBN 978-0-7528-8412-7

Printed and bound in Great Britain by Clays Ltd, St Ives plc

www.orionbooks.co.uk

This book is dedicated to all those victims who never had the chance to be survivors, to my wonderful mother, Sandra Luby – I got him for all of us – and to my supportive, loving, wonderful family.

CONTENTS

Acknowledgements

I would like to thank all those people who had faith and belief in me:

Amanda Harris and Anna Valentine from Orion, for their reassurances and commitment to me, especially when I felt the dream would never be a reality. Thank you for spurring me on through my wobbly moments.

Thank you to Jean Ritchie, for your chocolates, cards, many hours of patience in writing this book, our playful times with Jet the cat and dreams of losing weight, ha, ha. You made writing this book easy.

To Marian Levy from Victim Contact Unit and Lionel Copes from the Crown Prosecution Service.

DS Peter Cain from Liverpool Police and Sue Smith, a good mate from National Children's Homes.

To members of my family and extended family:

Gordon and Anne Luby, always there no matter what. Edward Costain, my real dad, Doreen and Henry Jones, and Irene McGovern, my lovely ma-in-law. Thank you for hours of listening.

To my soul sister Donna Daniels and her family. Thank you, friend. Our secrets lasted forty years, and you never let me down. I love you, Donna.

To Mick, David, Gordon, Courtney, Joanne and baby Abi, my very own little family. I worship you all. Love conquers all.

Our family life is wonderful, and I thank you for believing in me and supporting me.

To my two brothers and their families. Thank you for believing in me and giving the support every sister needs. I love you both for ever.

Last but not least I thank God for standing beside me, and Jesus for giving me the strength when I felt abandoned and afraid. My faith never faltered.

'MENTAL/PHYSICAL'

A poem started when I was a child and finished when I was
in my thirties.

The window without a view from which I stare each day
Shows nothing but blank spaces, while children outside play.
But me, I feel so different you can see it in my eyes.
I didn't dare to tell the truth in a silence filled with lies.
I know how I loved him, and I thought he loved me too,
Until one night, in awesome fright, he bruised me through and
  through.
He raped my mind and body, and made me scared of things to
  come.
I was buried in dark shadows and could not reach my mum.
He thinks he's got away with it, but one day he will pay.
It happened many years ago and it's time I had my say,
How I hate my stepdad, and I realise he's no good,
He's never been repentant, or even understood.
Why should I be punished? Why should I take the blame?
Or be silenced by convention, to suit the adult game?
Now I'm a woman, fully grown, and my story must be believed:
Daddy stole my virginity, and he's never even grieved.
He ravished my mind and body, and he pandered to his lust,
Then left me as a lifeless doll, as all paedophiles must.
Now I hate my daddy, and the cross he's nailed to me.
I've exorcised my ghosts, and finally I am free.

*Though I'll never find the innocence that was robbed from my
    childhood bed,
Never know who I should have been, or the life I may have led,
I found a strength that was deep within
To survive this monster and not let him in.
So if you understand me, please understand my pain.
Don't let your past rape you once again.
Be proud of who you are and what you have achieved.
I can feel your pain, and yes, you are believed.
You are a wonderful person, you've survived and you've pulled
    through.
There's only one thing now you have to understand:
Everyone loves you.*

INTRODUCTION

In my mind, I am sitting on the pavement with my best friend Donna. Between us lies a pile of daisies we have picked in the park, and we are carefully threading them on to a daisy chain. She is working at one end, and I the other. Soon we will bring the two ends together and join them in a big circle.

But that will not be until my stepfather has stopped raping me. When he has hauled his heavy, sweating bulk off my eight-year-old body, I will, in my imagination, thread together the last beautiful link. The daisy chain will then be whole, complete. And so will I. My mind will once again have carried me away from the torture being inflicted on my small body.

Living in my imagination is how, from the age of four to seventeen, I survived the constant and brutal abuse my stepfather inflicted on me. He raped and damaged my body, but he was never able to get inside my head, to my daisy-chain world.

Today, forty years on, my stepfather is serving a long sentence in prison. I put him there.

Now my life, like the daisy chain, is complete.

CHAPTER ONE

The first four years of my life were very happy, which was surprising, considering that my birth was not planned or wanted.

My nan was a respectable, hard-working woman and was shocked and ashamed when her fifteen-year-old daughter, Sandra, tearfully confessed she was pregnant. My granddad, Frank Luby, was a seaman and was away on a Cunard liner when Mum broke the news to Nan. In those days there was no means of contacting him. Besides, there was little point: both Nan and Mum knew he would be furious.

At first Nan was determined to report my dad to the police for having sex under age. Dad, Eddie Costain, was only a couple of years older than Mum, and they were both very young and naïve. In the end, my nan said that if I was born after Mum turned sixteen, she would not go to the police. I saved Dad's bacon by arriving on 22 March 1960, three weeks and a day after Mum's birthday. The minute I kicked and bawled my way into the world, I found a place in my nan's heart; all her anger and shame were instantly forgotten. She really loved me, and I have never in my life felt more cherished and secure than when I was with her.

In the early stages of the pregnancy, while Granddad was still at sea, Mum was so afraid of how he would react that she went to a backstreet abortionist to get rid of me. She was the apple of his eye and couldn't bear to think of how hurt and angry he would be, so she took the £10 that Nan had put aside to buy things for the baby, along with a bit of money she had saved herself, and found a woman who was prepared to do it. But the smell of alcohol on the woman's breath and the sight of blood on her apron were terrifying. She muttered an excuse about needing to get some more money and fled.

'I took one look at that blood,' she told me years later, 'and reality hit me. This woman could not only kill my baby, she could also kill me.'

She went straight to Woolworths and spent every penny on blue baby clothes, convinced she was carrying a boy. When she told me, she laughed, saying, 'I should have known that whatever I wanted, I would get the opposite as a punishment.'

Although I never doubted my mum's love for me, I was always aware that I was, at least in the beginning, second best. But she went through a lot to have me: I know that when Granddad eventually came back from sea, he gave her a beating for getting herself pregnant, and she was made to feel she had let the whole family down, a feeling that was only alleviated when she and Dad were married, three months after I was born.

We lived in Liverpool, in the Lark Lane area. Today, it's a place of trendy bistros and wine bars, but back then, in 1960, it was poor. The small two-up, two-down terraced houses on and around Lark Lane had originally been built to accommodate the servants who worked for the big houses in nearby roads, where the ship owners and merchants who made their fortunes in Liverpool's port had lived. At the end of Lark Lane was Sefton Park, one of the biggest and most beautiful open spaces in Liverpool, with bridle paths round it for the gentry to exercise their horses. If you climbed the large stone wall that separated Lark Lane's terraces from the big houses, you could look down on manicured lawns and orchards. But by the 1960s everything was changing: many of the big houses were being split into flats, and the small terraced houses were inhabited by working-class families struggling to get by.

Granddad was a shadowy presence in my childhood because of his long absences at sea, but I remember him as strict and loving. Nan was very much in charge of the family. Mum was the eldest of three: she had a brother, Frank, and a brother, Gordon, the youngest, who was only seven years older than me. Gordon was a very important figure in my childhood and my life as a whole. He was a constant, dependable, loving force for good.

Mum was a beauty, a five-foot-two-inch blonde with a peaches and cream complexion, a real head-turner. Dad, too, was a good-looking young man, small and dark-haired. He worked in the docks, but in the evenings played in a band. One of his mates in the music business was Gerry Marsden, who was destined to achieve fame in Gerry and the Pacemakers. There's a story in the family that Dad was offered the chance to join that group but Mum was fed up with him being out in pubs and clubs in the evenings, and knew other girls would be making a play for him, so she put her foot down and refused to let him. Looking back, we can probably all see points in our lives where, if another path had been followed, things would have worked out very differently. This was one in mine as well as my dad's.

Mum and Dad were happy together at first. They had a flat at the top of one of the big houses in Parkfield Road. It was just five minutes' walk from Nan's terraced house in Aigburth View, off Lark Lane, and my early years were divided between the two places. We only lived in Parkfield Road for about eighteen months, but my first clear memory is of life there. It was a lovely, sunny day and I was in front of the house in my pram, a big Silver Cross, which we kept for years. In those days it was quite normal for babies to be left outside to get some fresh air, and I was harnessed into the pram. I remember Mum calling to me from the top window to look for Daddy coming home from work, and I can picture him turning the corner and walking towards me. Next to my pram was a hedge, which was interlaced with roses, and I recall stretching out my hand to get one of the pretty flowers. I grabbed the stem, and the thorns tore into my chubby pink palm. I screamed and Dad ran as fast as he could towards me, scooped me up and hurtled upstairs, yelling at Mum to be more careful.

The rose incident must have happened at about the time that my brother Tom was born. He is eighteen months younger than me, and I fell in love with him from the second I saw him. He was a blond, wriggly baby with a ready smile, the greatest gift anyone could have given me. As he grew, we became a close little team.

My best friend, then and throughout my life, was Donna Daniels, who was born six months after me to Mum's good friend Margaret. Our two family dynasties were intertwined: Nan and Donna's grandmother were best friends, Mum and Margaret were best friends, my dad played football with Donna's dad, and then Donna and I became inseparable. Our mums and dads used to take us to the park for family picnics together, and Donna and I grew up as close as sisters. Donna had two younger brothers, and with Tom they formed the core of our own little gang, added to by the other children whose lives ebbed and flowed around ours in the tight-knit streets – a happy band of urchins with runny noses, scabs on our knees and jam staining our faces.

Donna's nan Mary was a real character, a tough little woman who always seemed to be wearing a hairnet and rollers. She never walked, but bustled about at a run. I can picture her now, chasing me and Donna up the street with a brush in her hand to wallop us, because we'd been making a nuisance of ourselves, probably sticking our fingers into her jam or helping ourselves to biscuits.

It was a safe community for children: there was scarcely any traffic, we never saw strangers, doors were never locked, and everyone along Lark Lane and the streets off it knew us. We saw more horses than we did cars; there was one that pulled the milk churns up to the dairy, another with the heavy coal cart and a third owned by the rag-and-bone man, who, if we were lucky, would give us balloons. Nan was frightened of the horses and would grab my hand. 'Keep away from them things,' she'd say. There was also a pig farm further along Lark Lane, at the place we called the dairy. (There were no cows, but the big stainless-steel milk churns were delivered there.) Sometimes, to the delight of us kids, the pigs would be run down the street.

Best of all, at the end of the lane was Sefton Park, the greatest playground in the world. As young as three or four years old, we were allowed to wander up there on our own to play. I was given threepence a week in pocket money, and it would all be spent at Mrs Pearson's sweetshop, usually on Walkers' toffee, my favourite. Across the road was Joe's café (now a Chinese restaurant), which had a snooker table and a row of pinball machines. I used to sneak in to watch Uncle Gordon play the machines, until the owner spotted me and chased me out.

When we had snow, there would be huge snowball fights in the street, with the dads joining the children. At New Year everyone poured out of their houses to sing 'Auld Lang Syne' in a chain that stretched the length of Lark Lane, and we children spilled from house to house eating as much as we could stuff into ourselves.

After Tom was born, Granddad and Nan scraped together

the money to buy a house for Mum and Dad; in those days property was relatively cheap, and they paid a couple of hundred pounds, which was still a lot to them. It was an unusual house, in Hesketh Street, another tributary of Lark Lane, and even nearer to Nan's home. It had at one time been joined to a big house as servants' quarters, and it consisted of just three rooms, one on top of the other. On the ground floor was the living room, with a blue curtain across a small area that housed the sink and a door to the toilet. The cooker was inside a cupboard next to the fireplace. On the first floor was Mum and Dad's bedroom, and above it mine and Tom's.

Mum was a great homemaker, and she put a lot of effort into keeping everywhere clean and neat, using Cardinal Red polish on the front steps and windowsills. There was always a lovely smell of lavender from the furniture polish she used. She was very proud of her 1960s décor: purple floral wallpaper and lilac scatter cushions. My early memories of living there are of music constantly playing – it was the heyday of the Liverpool sound – Mum dancing while she did the housework, and Dad sneaking up behind and tickling her until they both collapsed laughing.

Round the corner at Nan's was my second home, and I think I spent almost as much time there as I did at our house, especially when Tom was very small. Another snapshot memory from my young life is of sitting on a bucket with my nappy off as Nan tried to potty-train me.

Life at Nan's was lovely. We would play Snap for hours and watch *Coronation Street*. She'd make me sugar or jam butties, and I'd drink 'connie onnie' (condensed milk). Her favourite tipple was sherry, and she'd smuggle me under her coat down to the off-licence, trying to get past Mum's house without her seeing us.

'Keep quiet while we're going past your house – your mum

will go mad if she knows I'm going out to get a bottle of sherry,' she'd whisper.

We'd buy packets of crisps and sneak back for our cosy evening together. Then I'd sleep with her in her soft double bed with a big dip in the middle. I would wake up in the morning in the centre of the ancient mattress, with Nan's arms round me. Then we'd go downstairs and Nan would get the kettle on and light the fire.

Her elder son, Frank, had left home by this time and I don't have many memories of him, but Gordon was about ten and she'd battle to get him up for school. I can remember her shouting, 'Gordon, get out of that bed or I'm coming up there with a bucket of water and a soggy flannel!'

Gordon would put his feet out of the bed and bang them up and down on the floor to sound as if he was walking about. 'I'm up! I'm up!' he'd yell.

Then me and Nan would settle down to tea and toast in the kitchen. Later, when Tom was bigger, he'd join me at Nan's when Mum was working; she always had cleaning jobs, and at one time worked as an usherette at the local Odeon cinema. I own up to being a little bit jealous of Tom coming into my territory at Nan's, but not for long. I loved him too much.

When we deserved it, Tom and I would occasionally get a clip round the ear or a smack on our backsides. We could be naughty. For example, every day Mum would make up a 'carry-out' (a packed lunch) for Dad of sandwiches, a couple of biscuits and a piece of fruit to take with him to work at the docks. While he was finishing his breakfast, Tom and I would sneak into his workbag, open the box and take out the biscuits or the fruit. When we got really cocky and took his sandwiches as well, he came home fuming. 'I've had nothing to eat all day. Them little buggers have had my dinner!' After that, he made sure he checked it before he left the house.

He was a hands-on dad. When we were really small, he bathed us in the sink, but when we got bigger, we had an enamel bath that hung on the wall and would be filled with steaming water and placed in front of the fire.

Looking back, I can see that we were poor and money was tight, but because Granddad and Dad always worked, compared to many of the people in the area we were very comfortable. We had to put coats on our beds at night because we didn't have enough blankets, and we didn't have carpet in the bedrooms at home, but we were never hungry and Mum always kept me and Tom well dressed. Most of all, I was loved.

Not long after my fourth birthday, however, the laughter and music stopped. Things changed so slowly that at first I didn't notice anything was different, but then my parents began to row loudly. Dad was a jack-the-lad, young and immature, wanting to go out and have a good time, while Mum was at home, saddled with two little children. They were both so young, two kids catapulted into playing at being grown-ups. The arguments grew louder. Mum accused Dad of messing around with other girls; he denied it. Once, when he had stayed out all night, she attacked him with a frying pan.

I felt confused and miserable, but I didn't understand what was happening. One day Dad pulled me to sit on his knee and tried to get Tom to sit on his other one, but Tom wanted to go out and play, so he wriggled away. Dad solemnly told me that he loved us and would always be there for us. It was strange: we didn't make speeches like that in our family.

Mum shouted, 'No, you won't always be there! Don't go trying to get them on your side.'

Dad shrugged and just said, 'Please always remember I love you.'

Tom had escaped out of the door to play and I, with no idea

of the significance of the occasion, wanted to join him. 'Can I go out now?'

Dad laughed. 'Yeah, 'course you can.'

One afternoon a few days later I was sitting on the pavement outside our house with Donna when Dad came out carrying a large holdall. I knew something was wrong; he only ever had his small workbag.

'Where are you going?' I demanded.

'To the shops.'

I looked at his bag sceptically. It was bulging, and I could see through the broken zip that it was full of clothes.

'Why're you taking them clothes?'

'I'm dropping them at the laundry for your mum.'

I knew that couldn't be right. Dad never did the laundry; Mum used to pile it all on the old Silver Cross pram and push it to the launderette. I let out a wail, sensing that something was seriously wrong. He put the bag down, squatted to my level and held me gently in front of him by the shoulders.

'Now, you be a good, big girl for your mum and I'll see you later,' he said seriously. There was a funny catch in his voice and I started to panic.

Just then Tom came hurtling out of the house, his chubby two-and-a-half-year-old legs propelling him at top speed. 'Daddy, Daddy,' he shouted, and threw himself into Dad's arms.

Tears trickled down Dad's face as he hugged us close, kissed us, then got up and slowly walked away with his bag. He never turned round.

Tom was still crying out for Dad. I felt like crying too, but I had been told to be a good, big girl, so I hugged Tom and fished in my pocket for a lollipop that I had been licking all day. It took a few tugs to release it from my pocket, where it was stuck hard, and when it came out it was covered in fluff. I gave it a quick suck to get the bits off it and then popped it in

Tom's mouth. He was delighted and toddled away quite happy, all drama forgotten.

Although Dad had gone and we missed him, life was good for the next few months. We spent more time with Nan because Mum worked more, and we saw Dad every weekend. His own family life had been very sad: his father had died when he was young, and his mother had gone blind. She was still alive when I was born, and apparently she held me and ran her fingers over my face and cried, but she died soon after and I have no memories of her. Because of his mother's sight problems, Dad, who was an only child, had more or less been brought up by his auntie Ena and auntie Rhoda, who shared a house about twenty minutes' walk from where we lived. They were lovely, and when he split from Mum, he moved back in with them. Every Saturday he would pick us up and take us there. We'd always have a bath as they had a proper bathroom, which was a big thrill for us. Then they would give us orange juice and sandwiches and biscuits. Dad would play games with us and read stories.

For a time we had the best of both worlds. We loved our visits to the aunties, we loved our extra time with Nan, and Mum seemed happy again, with music once more playing in the house. We were too young to appreciate the sadness of Mum and Dad splitting up.

Years later Mum told me that she and Dad had signed up to be 'Ten-Pound Poms', to join the wave of British citizens who were encouraged to emigrate to Australia with low-cost fares. At the last minute Mum changed her mind and withdrew their application. It was another of those pivotal moments in my life. I'm not saying that moving to Australia would have saved Mum and Dad's marriage, but it doubtless would have saved me from the horrors that were just around the corner.

CHAPTER TWO

The day my world changed was a bright September day in 1964. I was four and a half years old and was at Nan's, having something to eat, when Donna called round to see if I wanted to play. I nodded eagerly and we walked hand in hand to Hesketh Street to play near our house. As I looked down the street, I saw Mum turn the corner with a big man by her side. To me, he was a giant, all six feet three inches of him towering over Mum's five feet two. He was not just tall, he was broad, with ginger hair and a really big nose. As I got closer, I saw that the words 'LOVE' and 'HATE' were tattooed on his knuckles. I didn't like him on sight, and Donna felt the same.

Mum introduced him a little nervously: 'This is my friend Mick Garvey.'

The first thing I noticed was that he spoke funny. He came from Luton, and to us little Scousers his Southern accent sounded foreign and weird. His voice was both loud and gruff at the same time, and I soon discovered that his manner was to bark orders, never to ask politely for anything. 'Sandra, get me a cup of tea,' was how he addressed Mum.

They had met when he was in a young offenders' institution about fifteen minutes' walk from where we lived. Mum and a couple of friends had walked past him sitting on the wall with some of his mates. They'd got chatting, and when he'd got out they'd met up again later. I think part of the attraction was that he was bad. Mum, who was twenty at the time, had only just split from Dad. Mick was a couple of years older.

At first he stayed at our house only for the odd night, so his presence didn't impinge on our day-to-day existence too much. He was part of Mum's life, but not ours. But gradually he began to spend more and more time in Hesketh Street and one fateful day he moved in. I discovered later that he was a long-distance lorry driver and had a family back in Luton. When his wife (I don't know if they were legally married) had found out about Mum, she'd kicked him out, which was why he moved in with us full-time.

There were brief reprieves when he went away in his lorry for a few days at a time, but after Mick had moved in, things at home suddenly changed for the worse. Little by little he invaded every aspect of our lives. If he was home, Tom and I had to keep the noise down. We learned to tiptoe around him. We weren't allowed to sit on *his* chair; I can remember wondering why he had to have his own special chair when everyone else just shared. Then he started to take over our family with his rules. He'd say things like, 'You should be giving these two a bit more discipline, Sandra.' At first it sounded as if he cared about us, and was doing it for our own good. 'Those two are running wild – you shouldn't let them stay out so late.' But it wasn't because he cared; it was to do with control, a speciality of his. He always needed to be in control, and he made sure he was.

One of the first things he did was try to stop me spending so much time at Nan's. She had hated him on first meeting, and he caused endless arguments between her and Mum – so much so that for a time they didn't speak to each other. But I ignored his ban, and always found a way to sneak round to Nan's house.

He swore every other word. We came from an area where swearing was normal – we'd heard all the words before, but to hear them bellowed from the mouth of a huge man with a rough voice in our own home was frightening and horrible. His voice made him sound as though he was telling us off, even if he wasn't.

He tried to make the whole family into his slaves. Tom and I had to sit at his feet, tickling them for hours on end while he sat there with a fag in one hand and a mug of tea in the other and watched TV. If we stopped because our arms ached, he'd command us to use our other hand.

The music in the house stopped when he was around, and when he was away, Mum started to play sad songs, like Engelbert Humperdinck's 'Please Release Me'. She became nervous and tense. We all walked on eggshells. If I was playing out in the street and I heard that booming voice – 'Sharon!' – I'd jump up immediately and run.

Near Christmas, a couple of months after he'd moved in, Tom and I were in bed at the top of the house when we heard a lot of shouting in the street. We instantly recognised Mick Garvey's distinctive voice. We peered out of our window, and in the light from the streetlamps we could make out our dad in the middle of the road with a pile of gaudily wrapped Christmas presents in his arms.

'Please,' he was saying wearily, 'I only want the kids to have their presents from me. I'll give them to Sandra. Surely that isn't too much to ask?'

Mick Garvey let out a roar and lunged towards Dad, punching him in the face and scattering the presents across the wet road. He stamped on every one, smashing the contents to pieces, then ran at Dad again and started to beat him up. It was a chilling sight and Tom and I watched numb with shock as our father was beaten to the ground. Mick Garvey was almost a foot taller than Dad, and a much bigger build. He kicked and

punched him until my poor dad picked himself up, ran up the
road and left our lives, with Mick Garvey shouting after him,
'Don't you set foot near my Sandra and the kids ever again or
I'll really do you.'

In desperation I was shouting, 'Dad! Dad!' from the
window, but he didn't hear me. He just kept running. The
weekend visits stopped and we didn't see Dad for a long,
long time.

That night, Tom and I climbed into the same bed and clung
together as we sobbed ourselves to sleep. We knew, with
absolute certainty, that our dad would not be able to rescue us
from this monster who had invaded our home. The next
morning I looked out of the window and saw that our broken
toys and torn wrapping paper had been cleaned from the street.
It was as if nothing had happened. Little did I know that this
was only the beginning.

A few weeks later, not long after Christmas, Mick sat me on
his knee and pretended to tickle me. He forced my buttocks
deep into his lap, digging his fingers into my waist to hold me
down. I started to struggle to free myself, but he tightened his
grip, saying, 'I'm only trying to give you a cuddle.'

I carried on wriggling, but Mum, who was in the same
room, said, 'Aw, Sharon, he's only trying to give you a love.'

He jiggled me up and down as if playing with me, but I felt
very uncomfortable with the way he was rubbing me, even
though I didn't know why. As his big hands drove me down on
to his lap, I felt movement under my buttocks; something hard
was digging into me. His breathing grew heavier and he
clenched his teeth together so fiercely that I could hear a
grinding noise.

This was the first of many times, and it happened even if
Mum was in the room, cooking dinner with her back to us. I

knew he enjoyed inflicting pain on me, though I didn't understand why. I sensed there was something wrong, and I hated it. I did everything I could to make sure I was never near enough for him to grab me, but he always managed it.

Afterwards, he'd say things to Mum like, 'I'm only trying to be affectionate, to show her I love her,' and this made me feel worse, because to me it seemed that what he was doing was OK with Mum, so it must be my fault that I didn't like it.

I had no idea about a man's body. I knew what a little boy like Tom looked like, but I had never seen my dad without his boxer shorts. I was completely confused by what Mick was hurting me with, but I soon found out it would be worse if I didn't humour him.

It was about this time, after he'd been in our home for a few months, that he began to beat Mum. For no reason at all he would start screaming, 'You're a whore. Who are you seeing?'

Mum would cower and beg, 'Please, Mick, you know I love you. I would never look at anyone else.'

Impervious to her pleas, he would start punching and kicking her all over the tiny living room, growling, 'Get upstairs, you pair of idiot bastards,' at me and Tom.

We would run upstairs as fast as we could, terrified that he was going to kill our mum. Sometimes, when he was really laying into her, Mum would manage to escape out of the front door and run to a neighbour's house, but Mick would bang their door down and drag her back by her hair, hurling abuse and threats at anyone who tried to stop him.

He didn't care who saw him attacking Mum – he'd do it in the pub or in the street. If anyone tried to stop him, he'd beat them up too. He was a bully, and nature had given him the big frame and the strong arm to allow him to be one.

He soon imposed his presence on the neighbourhood. All the kids in the street were scared of him, and none of the men would stand up to him. He was opinionated, and when he was in the pub, he'd hold forth and nobody would dare contradict him, even if he was wrong. He'd shout them down, a big, physically strong man with a loud voice: you couldn't argue with him.

He was well known in both the local pubs, the Royal Masonic and the Albert on Lark Lane. He was the kind of man who would pick up his lorry-driving wages and buy drinks for everyone in the bar and have nothing left to give Mum. He could be as nice as pie with other people, although those who knew him quickly got the measure of him. But they walked on eggshells like we did; if Mum's friends didn't talk to him, he beat her up for turning them against him. So they kept the peace, for her sake.

Once, when he was beating her up, she escaped and ran up an alleyway. I was out in the street and saw it all. He ran after her, and because she was trying to look behind her, she ran full tilt into a broken, rusty wheelbarrow that someone had dumped there. She split her knee wide open. I ran to her and gaped at her knee in horror. It was as if I could see right inside her body: muscles, ligaments, bone. Mick Garvey stopped in his tracks and, with a look of panic on his face, picked her up and carried her back to our house, lying her down on the floor. Even then, he was blaming her: 'If you had fucking done what I fucking told you in the beginning...'

We were ordered up to bed, and I lay there shivering for hours, thinking Mum would be dead in the morning. I don't know if she went to hospital – I was only little and can't recall all the details – but the next day she was hobbling around with her leg bandaged. I was so relieved that she was OK.

Mick was more violent when he was drunk, but he didn't need drink to start his attacks. Mum was always trying to appease him, but I realised later that he would often start fights in order to go out. He was a womaniser and would make sure he had his chance to go out without her by beating her so hard she could barely move.

Sometimes he'd come in to a clean house and she would be busy ironing his shirts and have a meal ready for him, yet he'd carefully run his fingers over the top of the doorframe. If he picked up any dirt, he'd shout, 'This place is a shit hole and I'm not staying here.' Then he'd take one of the freshly ironed shirts and storm out.

Many nights we lay in our beds at the top of the house listening to them arguing and Mum screaming as he kicked and punched her. The worst bit was the silence after the screams, which terrified me because I would be sure that he had killed her.

It wasn't long before the violence towards me and Tom began, although I think I always got the worst of it. I don't want to diminish what Tom suffered, because it was terrible, but I think Mick Garvey was sly enough to realise that small boys grow into big men, and that he was better off exploiting his sadistic streak on the two females in the family.

To punish me and Tom, he'd take off his belt and put us over his knee, trousers pulled down, and leather us. The first time it happened was a real shock: we'd had the odd slap on our hands or the backs of our legs from Mum, but nothing like this violence. Nothing we ever did warranted the brutality of his beatings. If he had me on his own, after the thrashing he would rub the weals that came up on my bottom, something he never did if Tom was there. If Mum was home, he'd take us to the top floor of the house, telling her that he was going to give us a slap. By the time we reached our bedroom, his belt would be off and we both knew what was coming. I remember lying across his lap watching my tears splash on the floorboards. I never dared to cry out loud, because that made it worse. For

me, it was easier when Tom was there, because it was over
more quickly, and there would be no rubbing and touching
afterwards.

When Mick was in the house, I had at least one beating a
week. I couldn't answer back, even if he was accusing me of
things I hadn't done. When Mum and Dad had been together,
Tom and I had been allowed to speak freely; now we had to
creep around in silence, hoping not to upset him. And he was
clever with his violence, too. He would leave Mum with black
eyes and bruises, but with us kids he was always careful to
thump in the stomach, the backside, the back, the tops of the
legs or across the head, where it wouldn't show. Mum had no
idea how violent he was towards us, because the bruises that
came up on our backsides didn't show when our trousers were
pulled up. In the street, he would grab me by my hair and kick
me all the way home. To this day, my bottom is numb in parts,
and pulling my hair doesn't hurt me, because I became so
used to it.

He would casually pinch the inside of my arm as he walked
past me, even if I had done nothing wrong and was sitting
quietly, trying not to be noticed. It would be with such strength
that I would have a massive bruise afterwards. Back in the
1960s a 'domestic', which involved 'showing the wife who's the
boss', was something society turned a blind eye to, but physically beating children could lead to trouble. The fact that he was
so careful shows that, even in his rage, he was in control.
Control was his watchword; he wanted power and control over
all those around him and we were easy prey.

One of the worst things he did was to force me and Tom
to fight each other, like a dog fight. It only happened when
Mum wasn't there, and it seemed to give him great
amusement. We'd be forced to hit each other, and he'd yell at
us if we didn't do it hard. I was eighteen months older than

Tom, and when you are only three and four, that's a big difference. So it would be Tom who got the verbal mauling: 'You pansy. You're a little girl – even your sister can beat you...Go on, hit her, hit her hard.'

To me it would be, 'Hit him in the face. Hit him hard or I'll wallop you.'

God forgive me, but I did hit my adored little brother. I had no choice. Neither of us did. It never stopped us loving each other. We both understood that it wasn't us doing the hitting; it was the brutish puppet master who was pulling our strings.

Not long before my fifth birthday the abuse stepped up a gear. It was a Sunday evening, and Mum had been unwell all day because she and Mick had been out the night before and she had a hangover. We'd had our tea, and Mum was rushing around organising our clothes for the next day.

She said to me and Tom, 'Get your pyjamas and then I'll wash you.'

Mick said, 'Don't worry, I'll sort the kids out.' He took Tom behind the blue curtain and washed him, then put him on the settee. 'Come on, Sharon.'

I didn't want him washing me. The only people I wanted to wash me were my mum, my nan, my dad and his aunties. But I knew that if I didn't do as I was told, there would be trouble and Mum would get the worst of it, so I went behind the curtain with him but kept my pants on.

He washed my face, neck, ears and hands, and then he said, 'Take your pants off.'

'No,' I said immediately, suddenly afraid. When Mum washed me, she would only clean me thoroughly on bath night and on other nights, such as tonight, she would do what we called a 'top and tail' and just push the flannel down inside my pants very quickly.

'Sandra, I'm trying to clean her and she's playing me up,' Mick called through to Mum.

From the other side of the curtain Mum said, 'Do as you are told, Sharon, and get washed.'

Hearing this, I thought it must be OK to take off my knickers, so I slipped them down. Then he put soap on his hand, not the flannel, and started washing between my legs. Suddenly I felt a searing pain as he shoved his finger right inside me. I pushed him away as hard as I could, but he caught hold of my arms and said firmly, 'Don't panic – I'm only trying to make sure you are clean inside and out.'

I stopped struggling and let him do it again, but it made me feel very uncomfortable. Nobody else had ever washed me inside. Perhaps Mum and Dad don't know how to wash properly, I wondered to myself.

That was the start, and I wasn't yet five years old. After that, he would often volunteer to wash me. When he put his finger in me, I thought it was in my bottom: I was too small to know there was more than one opening. The pain was as if he had cut me open and all my insides were being stirred up. Afterwards, there was a terrible burning sensation whenever I went to wee, which occasionally lasted for days. At times I wouldn't be able to poo for a couple of days. Looking back, I can see it was psychological because I believed he had been inside my bottom. Mum would just assume I was constipated and give me orange juice.

When he washed me, he didn't restrict himself to putting his fingers inside me; sometimes he'd grab my hand and shove it down his pants and make me hold his 'thing', which was the name I gave to it. Then he'd put his hand over mine and move it up and down. Before long I realised that the faster it went, the sooner it would all be over. As he got more and more excited, he'd say, 'That's a real good wash you're having, darling. Oh, yes.' He'd have one hand clamped over mine and the other round me. If I made any noise, he quickly put his hand over my mouth.

Whenever Mum was out, he would be more open about it and he wouldn't restrict himself to doing it when washing me. He'd just unzip his trousers, take out the thing and make me rub it. I would think he had peed on me; I didn't know what it was. But I hated the sliminess of it on me. I never looked at him or it – I kept my eyes closed or turned my head to look at the floor or out of the window. I was frightened of the thing and didn't want to see it. Afterwards, he would be nice to me, saying things like, 'You're a good girl.' He'd use toilet roll to clean me up, and he'd sponge my clothes with a damp cloth if they were stained. Then he'd be nice to me, perhaps for the rest of the day, allowing me to go out to play and siding with me if I was arguing with Tom.

Then one day when I was six, he walked up the street to where Donna and I were playing and called me in. I can remember the day clearly: it was just before Donna's sixth birthday and she was going to have a party. I was both envious and excited at the same time, really looking forward to it.

Donna said to me, 'I'll wait on the step for you.'

'You piss off,' Mick grunted. 'She's not coming out again.'

Inside, he made me sit on a chair and knelt down in front of me, his face close enough for me to smell his aftershave and breath, which always stank of cigarettes and sometimes alcohol. There was something particularly menacing about him that day and I drew back from him.

'You listen to me,' he began in a low growl, 'you don't go telling anyone what happens in this house between me and you or me and your mother. Right?'

I nodded, terrified of what was going to happen next. Then he commanded me to take off all my clothes and lie on the floor. I did as I was told. He opened his trousers and spent the next half an hour enjoying himself, using me as his sex toy. I thought it would never end. He held my hips roughly, lowered his head and performed oral sex on me. He rubbed his thing all over my tummy and my nipples, and eventually he shuddered and finished. I remained on the floor, cold and shaking, until he took me behind the curtain, washed me, told me to get dressed, gave me a penny and sent me back out to play.

'Good girl,' he said. 'Go and buy a sweet.'

I stumbled out of the house, numb with fear. When I found Donna, she could tell something was wrong. I was pale and obviously in shock. 'He's done something bad,' I blurted out. 'He made me take my clothes off. He's messing with me.'

In Liverpool in the 1960s 'messing' with someone had definite sexual connotations. Although we were both too young to understand, Donna knew that something very wrong was happening to me and she burst into tears. I was upset that I had made her cry and, young as I was, decided never to burden her with any details. From then on, I'd tell her when he had been 'messing' with me, but never any more than that.

She often said, 'Sharon, can't we tell someone?' but I explained that he would kill my mother. I really believed he would; I had seen her lying on the floor with blood pouring from her face, and I knew that the slightest thing would set him off. I pleaded with Donna not to tell anyone, and although I felt relief at being able to share my dreadful secret, I was also scared that I couldn't be a hundred per cent sure that it was secure. Looking back, I should never have doubted Donna: she kept my secret safe.

As the months wore on, the sexual abuse became ever worse. He was always touching me. Sometimes he would send me upstairs as a punishment for some naughtiness I hadn't done and then follow me up a few minutes later. He'd say, 'Your mum says if you are a good girl you can come down. Have you been good?'

'Yes,' I'd reply timidly.

'No, you haven't – you haven't done this yet,' he'd respond, opening his trousers, pulling out the thing, and getting me to hold it and rub it. Then he'd let me back downstairs.

If Mum was at work in the evening, he'd come into the bedroom while Tom was asleep in the other bed, pull down my pyjamas and lie on top of me. He made no sound – although Tom was only four, he never risked waking him up. Whatever he was doing to me, one hand was always free to clasp instantly over my mouth if I made a noise. He'd put the thing between my legs and move it up and down; he'd kiss me on the lips and force his tongue into my mouth. I didn't understand what was happening or why, but I knew it was wrong because he only did it when mum wasn't there. I was afraid of him, and I don't know how I knew it, but I was aware that what was happening was shameful and a secret.

Sometimes he would lift me out of bed and carry me downstairs to play his games, away from the risk of waking Tom. Night after night I'd lie awake in bed, petrified that he would come in. Looking back, I spent half of my childhood waiting for something terrible to happen, and it almost always did. It could happen at any time and I knew it. I lived in constant fear of being left alone with him.

The jiggling up and down on his lap carried on, and there were times when I even volunteered for it, to stop him putting Tom on his lap. He'd say to Tom, 'Come and sit on my lap while we watch the football.' I'd rush over and push Tom out of the way. I didn't want him to have to go through that. As a threat, Mick would say that if I told anyone, nobody would believe me and I'd be taken away to a children's home. Chillingly he would add, 'And then I'll only have Tom to love.' I became really worried that he would hurt Tom in the way that he hurt me. I hated what he did to me, but I believed, in my very childish way, that it was my job to be abused and that I had to save Tom from it at all costs. He knew just how to manipulate me and he would take advantage of my fears countless times over the dark days to come.

CHAPTER THREE

Mick used every trick in the book to make sure that I would never trust anyone with his dirty secret. He told me, repeatedly, that nobody would ever believe me, and he worked hard at making sure they wouldn't. In clever ways he undermined my credibility, making me out to be a liar and not to be trusted. Once, he stormed into the house and dragged me to my feet, making me stand up straight in front of him.

Mum tried to calm him down. 'What's she done, Mick?'

'What she's done? She was swearing in the street and told a mate of mine to piss off when he came out of the boozer and refused to give her money, that's what she's done.'

It was a barefaced lie. I never begged, and I never hung around outside the pub.

'No, Mum,' I gasped, 'I never. It's a lie! I swear to God I never—'

Whack! The pain shot through my head as his fist connected with my temple.

'Calling me a fucking liar, are you?' he roared, his eyes blazing. 'You cheeky fucking bitch.'

Whack!

Mum grabbed hold of me, ran me up the stairs and told me to stay in my room. I lay on my bed, listening in horror to him beating her, and blaming myself. Why did this keep happening?

The next morning, before Mick got up, Mum said tiredly,

'Do me a favour, Sharon, don't keep upsetting him. Just agree with him, and please keep out of trouble.' She had a black eye and was walking stiffly.

This made me think that Mum believed I was a liar, that she believed I had been begging outside the pub. It was very clever of him: it reinforced in me the feeling that nobody would ever take my word against his, which was what he told me when we were on our own, and he'd say things like, 'Don't ever fucking tell anyone what I do to you, because they won't believe you and I'll kill your mother anyway.'

My feeling of isolation and entrapment only increased with time. One day he threw away all the bread in the bin and took it outside for the binmen. I thought, Why's he done that? I wanted a butty. But I knew better than to say anything.

When Mum came in, she said, 'Where's the bread?'

'Fatty here ate it all,' Mick said, rolling his eyes and gesturing at me.

'What, half a loaf?' Mum asked.

'Yeah, she was getting all her mates round and making sandwiches.'

When I protested and told Mum he'd put it in the bin, he said in mock surprise, 'You lying little cow.'

Once again, Mum believed him.

His biggest coup was one hot summer's day when I was six. I was playing in the street with Donna, pushing lolly sticks into the melting tar on the road. Mum was working at a dry-cleaner's in Lark Lane. I can remember the scene vividly: I was wearing a blue gingham dress, and my hair was tied up in pigtails. I was so engrossed in our game that I didn't notice Mick turning into Hesketh Street. Donna spotted him. She grabbed my arm and pulled me to my feet, running towards an alleyway.

'Quick,' she said, 'it's the Nutter.'

That was one of our secret names for him. Tom and I always referred to him as 'It'. I felt sick, and within seconds I heard that coarse voice bellowing my name.

'Don't go in – your mum's not at home,' Donna pleaded.

'It will be worse if I don't,' I replied. I saw her stricken face as I turned to walk towards him; sometimes I think she suffered almost as much as I did.

I was expecting to be abused when he pulled me inside the house, but this time things were different.

'You stole money from my pocket this morning,' he said calmly, as soon as the door was shut on the outside world.

'No I didn't.'

'Yes you did, you lying little bitch.' He turned and picked up Mum's favourite vase, a present from Nan, from the mantel-piece and smashed it on the floor.

I gasped. I thought, Mum's going to murder him now.

'Why did you do that, Sharon? Why did you break her vase?' he asked, his voice cold and calm.

'You done it!' I protested.

'Oh, did I?' he said. He grabbed my arm and dragged me out of the house.

We went up the road towards the dry-cleaner's where Mum worked, and I thought he was taking me there, but he hauled me past on the other side of the road. I could see Mum with her back to us, hanging clothes on the rail. I was willing her to turn round, but she didn't and we moved on. Then I thought he must be taking me to the park, but before we got there we came to the police station. He propelled me inside, his huge fingers digging painfully into my arm. He pushed me to one side and ordered me to sit on a bench. The local police all knew him and the desk sergeant looked up and said, 'Can I help, Mick?'

"Ello, mate. I've brought her here because me and her mum

are at our wits' end with her. She's started lying terrible. I noticed I had eight bob taken out of my jacket this morning. My missus wouldn't have taken it – I give her plenty and she only has to ask if she wants more. The only other person in the house was this one. Then she got angry before we left the house just now and broke her mother's best vase.'

The policeman looked at me gravely and said, 'Why did you do that, young lady?'

'I didn't,' I protested, willing him to believe me. 'I didn't steal the money or smash the vase.'

'See what I mean?' said Mick, sounding concerned. 'She's lying every day. We can't control her. Something's got to be done.'

The policeman came out from behind the desk, put his face close to mine and said, 'Are you going to tell the truth and apologise to your daddy?'

'No,' I said firmly. I knew I was telling the truth, and I felt sure the policeman would be able to see it.

He shook his head sorrowfully and said, 'Come with me. You'll see what happens to people who tell lies.' He took us through a door and down a corridor to the cells, and guided me in through an open door.

As I turned, I saw Mick standing behind the sergeant, a grin on his face that said, *Gotcha!*

'Right,' the policeman said, 'I want you to think about what you've done. I'm going to come back in a little while and I want the truth out of you.'

The door clanged shut and I could hear them talking as they walked away. There was a horrible stench in the cell, a mixture of pee, tobacco and disinfectant. In the corner was a bucket, and there was a small, bare bed, which I sat on. The walls were covered in writing, but I was too young to read it. I seemed to be in there, frozen and immobile, for a long time, but it was probably only ten or fifteen minutes. Then the policeman came in again.

'Are you going to tell the truth now?' he asked seriously.

'I am telling the truth. I didn't do it!' I pleaded, my eyes filling with tears.

'Do you want to go home and see your mum?'

'Yes,' I said in a small voice. My chin wobbled and tears ran down my cheeks. I wanted my mum so badly. I wanted to go home, go out to play. I couldn't understand it. I've done nothing wrong. Why am I here? I asked myself.

'Well, you are not going until you decide to tell the truth,' the policeman responded impatiently. 'I'll come back and ask you again.'

The door slammed closed once more and a wave of terror washed over me. I thought desperately, I have to live in here now.

After another ten minutes or so he returned, with Mick Garvey behind him. 'I'm going to ask you again and I want the truth this time. You will stay here until you tell the truth. Did you take the money and smash the vase?'

I gazed at him in despair and thought, If I tell the truth, I will never get out, but if I lie and say I did it, I can go home. None of it made any sense in my six-year-old head. How could lying be the right thing to do? I was very confused and started to cry again.

I heard the policeman sigh.

'OK, I did it,' I blurted.

'What did you spend the money on?' he asked.

I shrugged my shoulders. I didn't want to lie any more.

'If your dad brings you back here again, you will be going to a foster home,' he said as he escorted us out. 'I hope you've learned a lesson.'

I had, and a very bitter lesson it was too. In the grown-up

world, the truth was a lie, and a lie was the truth. I also knew
that I was helpless against Mick Garvey. On the way home, he
reinforced it.

'See, you little bitch, I've got the police in my hand, I've got
your mother in my hand, and everyone else in my hand. They
believe what I say. If you ever try to tell lies about me, you'll go
away and never be seen again. And if you try to make it hard,
I'll kill your mother and your brother. Do you understand?'

I felt trapped and just nodded mutely. Then he let me go
and play. I thought that was the end of it, but on the way home
he must have called in at Mum's work and told her of my
'crimes' because she came storming out of the shop and caught
up with me before I'd reached Donna's. She walloped me across
my backside and said furiously, 'Get in that house! You're not
going to Donna's. You're staying in.'

I heard Mick say in a caring voice, 'Sandra, let her go and
play. She's been punished.'

So there he was, presenting himself as the compassionate
dad. And my mum believed him. I realised he really did have
the power to turn Mum, the police, everyone against me. It was
a terrible, bitter realisation. Until that moment I had felt, deep
down, that Mum would side with me over him, but now I
knew that I was powerless and on my own.

It felt like I was trapped in a little hole and every day that
Mick lived with us the hole got bigger and I got smaller, until
I couldn't get out and the walls were towering over me.

We were surrounded by lies. There were the lies we were
all schooled to tell: a picture Nan had bought Mum for her
birthday was in the bin because he'd smashed it, but the line
we had to toe was that Mum had dropped it by accident. Her
black eyes and bruises were always caused by falling
downstairs or walking into doors. We lived in a world of
secrets and lies, but the secrets I had to keep were the worst.

Though I couldn't tell anyone, I certainly gave out plenty of clues that I was a very distressed and disturbed child. After the abuse became an established part of my life, I suddenly began to poo in strange places: right next to the toilet at Nan's and on the bedroom floor at our house. Looking back, I can see that I was demanding attention, silently begging those around me to look for the root cause of my problems. But naturally they thought I was being naughty and would punish me for my dirty and inexplicable behaviour.

Why did Mum stay with him? She loved and adored him, simple as that. God knows why, but she did. She'd been brought up in a close-knit community, and he was from outside, so was different. He was full of bullshit – promises about the wonderful life he was going to make for her. He fancied himself as a mobster, but in reality he was a minor criminal, a runner and hanger-on to some of the real big-time law breakers in Liverpool. He was never anything more than a plastic gangster, a wannabe.

To him, Mum was a trophy, a very pretty woman who had a loving family and good friends. And the more people around her disliked him and wanted her to leave him, the more determined he was to keep her in his web. He stopped her socialising with her friends and tried to keep her from her family. He used to say to her, 'They're jealous because you've got someone who will make something of himself. They're all stuck in Lark Lane in Liverpool with no prospects.'

School was a beacon of light and hope in my otherwise bleak existence. From the day I started, at around the age of five, until the day I left, many years later, I loved school. It was a haven, a place where I felt safe, and where I thrived.

Donna and I were in the same class at St Michael's Primary, we started on the same day, and we sat next to each other. I did well and always got good reports. I loved the fact that every dinnertime we were taken from the school in a long line, holding hands two abreast, across the road to the dinner hall. For some reason, being shepherded along safely by the teachers has stayed in my memory.

But it never mattered how good my day at school had been; on the way home, I was always very stressed and nervous. If I turned into our street and saw Mick's lorry there, or saw him standing on the doorstep, the terror would set in. All the way home I'd be offering up prayers: Please let Mum be home. Please, God, let Mum be home. Everything was better when she was there, but I could never predict when she would be, because of her cleaning jobs and part-time work. If she was there, he might grope me when her back was turned, but it was nothing compared to what happened when I was with him on my own. The best times of all were when he was completely off the scene, away with his lorry or, better still, in prison.

I don't know exactly what criminal scams he was involved in, but over the next few years he had a number of short stays in Walton Jail, the prison that serves Liverpool, for petty offences. Once, I saw him open a briefcase full of money and show it to Mum. But it wasn't his; he was holding it for someone else. Whenever he was inside Mum gave us strict instructions to tell the neighbours he was working away. Not that the neighbours were fooled: sometimes Tom and I only found out where he was when someone in the street told us. But he was only ever away for a few months.

I remember visiting him once. The jail was intimidating and we were all searched before we went in. I was thinking, This is the place he tells me I will come to if I ever let anyone know what he is doing to me. It's horrible.

I have no memory of seeing him in the visiting room, but when we were leaving, Mum told us to look up to where a handkerchief was being waved out of a window. 'That's him,' she said.

That night, and every night until he returned home, I prayed to God to keep him in there. And at the end of every day that he was away I would thank God for letting us have another peaceful day, a day when I didn't have butterflies in my stomach, and when I didn't peer into our road anxiously for his lorry when I came home from school.

Without the abuse and the bullying, I would have had a happy childhood. The children from the area all played together, and as the oldest of our little gang, I was always in charge, pushing the Silver Cross pram around with one or two toddlers in it. As soon as we were old enough, Donna's mum and my mum would load the pram with both families' washing and send us off to the launderette. Mum would ask me if I would do it and then add, 'I'm not asking, I'm telling.'

Sometimes Donna and I would be given picnics and told to take our younger brothers to the park. We'd have jam butties, a packet of Jammy Dodgers or custard creams and a bottle of pop. If we were lucky, there was money for ice cream.

We were often in trouble, and the police would come round to the house, but our 'crimes' were just naughtiness. We'd be caught scrumping apples from the houses with the big gardens, and once, me and Tom were hurling pieces of wood over a wall and had the bad luck to hit a policeman, who took us home to a leathering from Mick Garvey.

Donna and I developed a scam for getting money for sweets. We'd tell people in the street that we had lost our bus fare. It was quite successful for a while, until we became well known for it, so then we decided to knock on the doors of the posh houses in the next roads. We went up to a beautiful big house in Parkfield Road, and when a pleasant-looking middle-aged woman answered, I launched into my little speech. I was always the one who did the talking.

'Me and my sister, we've lost our bus fare, and if we don't get home, our dad will batter us. He'll take off his belt and beat us. He'll bang our heads on the wall and pull us around by the hair, and because I'm the eldest, I'll get it worst...'

Everything I said was based on what really did happen behind the closed doors of the house in Hesketh Street, but I could tell from the look of horror on the woman's face that I might have overdone it.

'Oh, my God...Come in,' she said, and showed us through into a large living room with leaded windows overlooking the garden. That one room was bigger than our whole house. She brought us orange juice and biscuits, and asked questions about the beating we would get.

I was warming to my theme, giving a graphic breakdown of the violence I experienced almost every day, when something made me realise that we were in deeper than we'd intended.

I didn't know how to get us both out, but I asked to go to the toilet, and she showed me one on the ground floor. I hastily climbed out through the window and found myself in the huge garden. The woman was sitting with her back to the window and Donna was facing it. I stood on the lawn, waving to her and signalling that she should get out. Donna's eyes widened in panic, and she told me afterwards that she felt sick. She said, 'I'll go and see where Sharon is,' intending to follow me out, but the woman went with her.

When the woman discovered I had gone, she said to Donna, 'I'm a social worker and I'm going to take you home because I think your father is abusing you. I'll get it stopped.'

Later, when Donna told me, I realised that I had passed up an opportunity to tell someone what was happening to me. On the other hand, though, if a social worker had turned up on our doorstep, Mick Garvey might well have murdered Mum. He would have been so furious he wouldn't have cared about the consequences.

The social worker drove Donna round to Lark Lane, and Donna had the presence of mind to give the wrong address. When the car stopped, she jumped out and legged it. I was waiting for her, having made my way back across the walls of the gardens.

I had missed my chance to end the nightmare.

Chapter Four

One day when I was eight years old, I was unwell and kept off school. I was determined to go, but I was running a fiery temperature and Mum insisted I stay home.

'You'll be all right. Mick's not working today, so he'll look after you,' she said, as she left for work.

'Can't I go to Nan's?' I begged.

'No, he'll think I don't trust him to look after you.'

I'd heard them arguing before and him saying, 'You don't trust me to look after them kids – what's the point of this relationship?' So I knew she was trying to avoid another fight.

I felt as though I was being fed to a lion. I knew it was inevitable that something would happen, however ill I felt. I was sitting on the couch, watching TV, when he came downstairs.

'It's just you and me, on our own all day. What are we going to do with ourselves?' he said with a leer.

'I'm going to do my homework,' I said, averting my eyes from him. There were butterflies churning in my stomach, as there always were when I knew that something was going to happen. A wave of nausea washed through me.

'No, you're not. You've got a day off school.' He sat down in his chair and watched TV.

I felt, for a brief moment, that I was going to be OK, because he hadn't come near me. I almost dared to believe that he would leave me alone because I was ill.

Then he said, 'Look what I've got. Come over here and sit with me.'

I turned and saw he had unfastened his trousers and the thing was in his hand. 'I don't want to,' I replied, knowing even as I said it that my defiance would not save me.

'Fucking come over here when I say,' he spat.

I knew better than to argue any more. I went over to him, praying silently that it would all be finished quickly. He made me kneel on the floor in front of him.

'I want you to suck it,' he said.

Disgust and shock surged through me. 'What?' I couldn't have anticipated this.

'Don't be fucking stupid.' He put his hands behind my head and forced me towards him. 'Open your mouth. Suck it. Suck it like you suck those round lollipops.'

No words can describe how vile this experience felt. I was sure he was murdering me. As he thrust into the back of my throat, I couldn't breathe. Surely I was dying. My stomach was heaving as if I was being sick, but my throat was blocked by his monstrous thing. At first my eyes were screwed tight shut – I always tried to shut my eyes, as if I could somehow block out the full horror of what was happening – but for some reason I decided to look at what was going to kill me. I opened my eyes and right in front of them was the thing. It was only a quick glimpse, but right there on his thing I saw a cross. I had always believed in God and seeing the cross was like a message from Jesus to tell me, 'I'm here for you. I will look after you.' A tiny glimmer of hope surged through me. As repulsive as the experience was, I felt Jesus was here for me and understood. I screwed my eyes shut again, confident that I would live, that I would survive this appalling ordeal.

After an eternity, he climaxed in my mouth and I vomited and vomited in the sink behind the curtain. Tears spilled from my eyes as my stomach heaved.

'Get washed and change your top,' he said. Then he washed my top and put it on the fireguard to dry, so that I was wearing it again when Mum came home.

From that day on oral sex was his regular way of abusing me, and he soon took to holding my mouth closed afterwards so that I was forced to swallow. I hated it more than anything and I was always sick and off my food afterwards. Mum used to say I was being 'awkward', refusing to eat her meals. I'd lie and say I'd eaten at Donna's.

If there was nobody around, he would talk dirty during the abuse, using vile language. He'd tell me I was a 'sexy little fucker' and a 'good wanker'. He'd then try to get me to say dirty words. I refused, and if he hit me, I'd just mumble something incomprehensible. He said menacingly, 'One day when I shag you, you'll be mine completely.' I didn't know what 'shag' meant, but I knew there was yet another ordeal in store for me.

There was no right way to behave when Mick was in the house. I'd try to stay quiet and out of his way, but if I went upstairs too early, before Tom was in bed, he'd follow me. He always had a plausible excuse for Mum: 'I'm going to make sure she's tidied that room' or 'I'm sure I can smell smoke on her.' Even as young as six or seven, he was accusing me of smoking, so that he could come upstairs and 'sort it out', which meant abusing me.

A few times Mum nearly caught him, but he was well attuned to the noises of the house, and if he heard a creak on the stairs, he quickly stopped. One night he had a narrow escape. He had waited until Mum was asleep before creeping into my bedroom and was lying over me. He had pulled off my pyjama bottoms and had his finger inside me.

Just then, from the floor below, Mum called out, 'Mick, where are you?'

He leaped up, hastily pulling up his tracksuit bottoms, and growled at me, 'Don't you say a word.' Then he shouted to Mum, 'It's all right, babe. She's had a nightmare and I'm just covering her up. I'll be back down now.'

I lay there thinking in despair, Oh, Mum, why did you call him? Why didn't you just come upstairs looking for him?

Another time he was nearly caught was when I'd just walked in from school. I went to our small kitchen area to make myself a jam butty, and he came up behind me, put his hand up my skirt, pulled my knickers down to my thighs and started rubbing me. He always spat on his hand for lubrication before he put his fingers up me, and it made me feel wet. I froze. I had a knife in my hand and for a brief moment I thought about turning and stabbing him, but I knew he was too strong to let me do it.

Just then I heard the front door open. The house had a tiny hallway, so he had only a second to pull away rapidly from me before Mum walked in. My knickers were still partly down under my skirt, and I stood stock still, praying she would sense something was wrong. Mum came across, took the knife and said she would make the butty. I went to the toilet and dried myself with toilet paper. It seemed nothing and no one could stop what was happening to me.

A flicker of light and happiness came into my otherwise bleak existence when my mum gave birth to my brother Phil when I was eight. Even though he was Mick Garvey's son, as far as Tom and I were concerned, he was the most fantastic gift. We adored him. Neither Tom nor I, and this goes right through our lives to the present day, have ever thought of him as having any connection to the monster. He was our brother, a full brother. We loved him, and we love him still.

When we were little, Mick treated Phil very differently to how he treated us. He adored his own son, spoiled him rotten. But Tom and I never minded, because we adored him too. He was so much younger than us that it was like having our own little pet. He was a golden child, well behaved and loving.

I can remember a family picnic in Sefton Park when Phil was about eight months old. We went with a friend of the family, Edie, and Mum and Mick. A blanket was spread on the grass for the baby to lie on, and Mick produced a large bag of soft sweets, which he put down next to Phil. Tom and I went to take one and our hands were smacked; they were Phil's sweets, and even though he was too small to eat them, we weren't allowed to touch them.

When I said, 'It's not fair – we haven't got none,' our stepfather replied, 'No, and you're not getting none. You're in the park – go and play.'

That's just one small example; every day Phil got preferential treatment. I don't remember ever seeing him being beaten, not even when he was older. We never held it against Phil, or felt any resentment towards him. But having him was a mixed blessing because Mick was so besotted with him that he spent more time at home.

I tried hard to keep the peace when he was around, I really did, but there was insecurity in just sitting in a room with him. If I sat quietly in a corner, he'd yell, 'What's up with you, you unsociable little bitch?' If I spoke or tried to appease him by making a fuss of Phil, I'd be accused of being 'nosy and inter-fering'. I could never relax at home. My bedroom was no refuge; if I went up there, he would follow and I would have to hold his thing or suck it. Sometimes he would squeeze my cheeks to force me to open my mouth; then he'd stick his tongue in and demand that I lick it. It was almost more disgusting than anything else, because it was so intimate. I hated the smell of his breath so close to me. (Years later, standing at a bus-stop in London, I smelled the same after-shave on a man near me in the queue and I went round to the back of the bus shelter and threw up.)

But I found ways to survive what was happening to me. Nobody ever taught me these strategies, they came to me instinctively and I believe they saved my life. They certainly saved my sanity. One of the worst things about life with Mick Garvey was that there was no pattern to it – he worked erratic-ally, and I never knew from one day to the next whether he would be home – so when I walked out of school at the end of each day, in my mind I would create a circle round me. The circle was my protection, and I lived inside it. It was like a force field, a barrier that nobody could penetrate, and inside I was safe. If I got home and he was there, or Mum said he was coming home that day, I'd keep the circle round me, and anything he did to me was to my body outside the circle: he could not get to the real me. If, on the other hand, Mum said he wasn't going to be home that night, I'd release the circle, like letting the air out of a balloon, and I could relax and feel comfortable without it.

Religion was another of my protections. I don't know where I first learned about God and Jesus – it's as if I always knew about them. My family was not particularly religious, although Nan and Mum were believers. I used to go to Sunday school with Donna, but it was her family who initiated it and I went along because she was going. It was there I heard the stories about Jesus and his love for everyone, even the least important people like me. Wherever it came from, I had a clear idea that God and Jesus were there to save me. I'd pray to God all the time, and as young as six one of my regular prayers was 'Please, God, make his lorry crash and kill him. Take him away from us, God.' Then I would be consumed with guilt and I'd pray for forgiveness. 'Please, God, I'm sorry for all the bad things I've been saying about him, but please just take him away.'

There was a church in Linnet Lane, and the door was always open. Me and Donna would go in there and talk to Jesus. Sometimes I went on my own. I always did a little curtsy in front of the altar, like I'd seen older people do, then I'd sit in the front pew and pour my heart out to Jesus. He was the only one I felt could share the full horrors of my life.

I said my prayers every night, and always thanked God for my life. In a strange sort of way, from a very early age I felt there was a purpose to my life, that one day I would do something to put all the bad things right.

I also tried to avoid being abused by keeping out of the house as much as possible. I'd go to Donna's or sneak to Nan's. But if Mick caught me, I'd quickly review the situation. Who else was in the house? Was someone likely to knock at the door? Can I get out before he realises I've escaped? If I couldn't, then my aim was always to get it over with as quickly as possible. I learned how to play the game, do what he wanted, satisfy him as fast as I could. And I learned my most important survival techniques.

A major technique was mentally to divide up my body. I felt that my body was his from the waist down and that part of me simply didn't exist. The middle bit contained my heart and my soul, and they were hurting, but the top bit, from my neck upwards, was mine, and he couldn't get in there. What happened in my head was nothing to do with him, and that's where I would retreat during the abuse.

When I was very young, I simply used to imagine something really nice while he was molesting me. In my head, I was walking down the road to the park, holding hands with either Nan or Mum, and in my other hand I had a coin to buy myself an ice cream. When we got to the park, we watched the riders cantering around the bridle path. It was a very simple little fantasy, but it kept me safe.

As the abuse got worse, I developed another scenario, my favourite. My imagination transported me to a pavement, where Donna and I were threading a pile of daisies onto a chain. As he abused me, I would be adding daisies one by one, and when he had finished, and only then, Donna and I would join our ends together and make a great big circle of daisies.

The third scenario was more macabre, and I used it for the worst times, when he was forcing me to have oral sex, when there was nobody around so he could take his time, or when I was feeling particularly low. In this one, I imagined I was being buried alive, standing upright in a deep grave. The soil was being shovelled in around me and would gradually cover my feet, my legs, my body. I'd count the seconds as the soil piled up, and I'd only start to panic if it reached my neck and throat before he had finished. Only once did I feel it was going to come up over my face and suffocate me, and on that occasion I suddenly lashed out in panic. Luckily, he finished at just that moment.

Salvation comes in the strangest of guises, and my mum had a friend, Henry, who, although he never knew it, was one of my greatest saviours. Henry was married to one of Mum's best friends, Doreen, a lovely lady who used to make us laugh because she swore all the time. 'I've tried to effing stop, but I effing can't!' she'd say. She and Mum were like twins – they looked alike, dressed alike and shared the same sense of humour. One thing they didn't share was their taste in men: Doreen's Henry was a kind, thoughtful man who provided well for his wife and daughters.

I remember as a child really envying Henry and Doreen's kids and wishing I could be part of their family. I thought their daughters were spoiled without knowing it, because they had so many things. I also envied Donna her family life; although her family was rough and ready and, like mine, never had much money, they were all loved and happy together.

When I was little, I couldn't say Henry's name properly and always called him 'Henbry'. He'd tease me: 'I haven't got a "b" in my name, you know.'

'I know, Henbry,' I'd reply.

What Henry did to save me was to introduce me to poetry. He wrote poems, and one day he read one out to me. I was only about six, but just hearing the way words could be strung together with rhythm and rhyme made a huge impact on me. I thought it amazing that people could take their feelings out of their body and put them on paper like that.

From then on I wrote poems. Simple little ones at first, getting better and better. I was so young when I started that I wasn't even doing joined-up writing. My poems were always very dark, because the subject matter of my life was dark. I couldn't write about sex, but I could write about pain and fear. I'd give them to Mum and she'd say, 'Can't you write about something more cheerful? They give me the shivers.' Later, I'd find my poem screwed up in a bin; at the time I was hurt, but I realise now I wrote so many she couldn't possibly keep them all.

Although I was a child, in many ways I had an adult brain. Because my abuser was treating me as a woman sexually, I developed mentally far ahead of my age, another factor that I believe was important in helping me to survive.

When I was nine, Nan became ill. I wasn't allowed to go and see her – Mick used her illness as an excuse to keep me away from her. She had gangrene in her foot and had to go into hospital to have her lower leg amputated. I was allowed to see her just before she went into hospital. She was standing outside her house, and she gave me a cuddle.

'When I come home, I'll be in a wheelchair, but I don't care if they take both my legs off as long as I can watch you grow up because you know I love you, don't you? It's not going to make no difference. Give your brothers a big kiss from me. See you when I get out.'

She never did get out. She had a massive heart attack and died on the operating table. She wasn't even fifty years old.

Learning of her death was a terrible shock. We were all being looked after at a neighbour's house, and when Mum got home from the hospital, she and Mick took us into our house and sat us down. Mum was crying so much that she couldn't tell us.

Mick said matter-of-factly, 'Right, your mum's too upset to tell you. I want you to be good for your mum because you know your nan had an operation?'

We nodded, concerned to see our mother so upset.

'Well, she died. She won't be coming back. Now go outside and let your mum have some peace.'

I was devastated. I felt my life was over, and I wanted to die with her. Uncle Gordon, only sixteen at the time, was distraught. I remember he tried to comfort me, but we were both so grief-stricken that all we could do was sob. Granddad came back from sea in time for the funeral, and he looked deflated, smaller and more tired-looking.

On the day of the funeral Mum said to me, 'Come with me to Rita's.'

Rita was a friend who lived a few doors up. We went inside. Mum and Rita were whispering together, and then Mum said to me, 'You stay here and I'll come and get you later.'

'I wanna come with you,' I pleaded.

'Behave yourself and stay here.' Then I heard her say quietly, 'Lock it, Rita, or she'll get out.'

I thought, She means me. Why am I being locked in?

Rita explained, 'Your mum just wants you to stay here with me until the funeral is over. Shall we have a cup of tea?'

'I'm going to see my nan...'

'No, you're not, lovely.'

About an hour later I heard noises from outside and went to the window. There were neighbours out in the street, and two big black cars were gliding slowly past. I could see the flower-laden coffin in the first car, and although nobody had explained it to me, I knew my nan was in that box. I screamed, 'Nan! Nan!' and hammered on the window. In the second car I could see Mum, Granddad, Uncle Frank, Uncle Gordon and Mick Garvey.

Why is he there? I asked myself. He doesn't belong there. He hated Nan and she hated him. I loved her. I should be there.

It was only when they returned for the wake that I was allowed out. I never forgave my mum for not letting me go to Nan's funeral, although I can perhaps understand that she was worried I would fling myself on the coffin.

After her death I substituted 'Nan' for 'God' in a lot of my prayers. I believed she was in Heaven looking down at me and would now be able to see everything that was happening to me.

'Please stop him, Nan,' I prayed. 'Please don't let him hurt me any more. Why did you have to go away and leave me and Mum?'

Granddad went back to sea after the funeral, and a couple of months later the council repossessed Nan's house. Gordon, who had been left on his own, had moved in with his girlfriend, Anne. Theirs truly is a match made in Heaven; they are still together today, great partners to each other and great friends to me. Throughout my life Gordon has been my shining example of what a man can and should be: a brilliant father and husband.

He is one of the very few people who ever tried to stand up to Mick Garvey. Once, after Mum had been badly beaten, with bruises and black eyes for the world to see, Gordon and one of his mates went round to our house. I don't know whether they managed to lay into Mick, but somebody called the police, and Gordon and his friend were arrested and held at the police station. Gordon was only eighteen or nineteen at the time. Mick wouldn't allow Mum to bail Gordon out. Thankfully, his girlfriend Anne's family were wonderful and came to the rescue; they became Gordon's second family.

When Nan's home was repossessed, the council sent some men with a van to clear out any possessions the family had not taken away. I saw them doing it and was furious that they were manhandling Nan's things, chucking her sideboard into the van as if it was a piece of old rubbish.

I ran up and started kicking one of the men. 'That's my nan's!' I shouted.

Mum came and pulled me off, gently asking me to go home. She could see how much I was hurting.

Less than a year after Nan died, Mum received a telegram to say that Granddad had died and been buried at sea. His employers, the Blue Funnel Shipping Company, offered Mum and Gordon a trip to sea to throw a wreath at the place where he was buried. Because Mick wasn't included in the trip, he refused to let Mum go, and without her Gordon was too young to go on his own. Gordon still feels bad about not having had the chance to honour his father in death.

A few months before Granddad's death we left Hesketh Street and the warm, supportive community of Lark Lane. It was the first of many moves. For some reason – probably to do with one of his court cases and his jail sentences – Mick Garvey owed a solicitor a lot of money. Anyway, he persuaded Mum to sign over the deeds of the house to clear the debt. Granddad, who had bought the house for Mum, was away at sea and didn't know what was going on. He probably wouldn't have been able to stop it; Mick always gave Granddad a wide berth, but if it had ever come to a real confrontation between them, Mick was much younger and bigger.

I was nearly ten when we moved to a rented bungalow in Heswall, another area of Liverpool. I had no idea where we were going or why, because in those days grown-ups never discussed their business with children. But I didn't want to go, and Donna and I had to be dragged away from each other, both of us crying hysterically. Donna wrote down her phone number and address, stuck the piece of paper in my pocket and told me to write and ring. I did, and have done ever since.

In a way, we had gone up in the world; Heswall was a posher area than we were used to, and the bungalow had a front and back garden. I can remember picking rhubarb from the rhubarb patch at the back. But it was a train and bus ride away from Lark Lane, from everyone we knew and all that was left of our family, and to us that may as well have been a million miles. We were isolated. Mum must have felt it even more than we did: Tom and I had each other, and baby Phil, to play with, but Mum knew nobody.

What's more, it wasn't the sort of area she could find work, and even if she could, there were no friends around to look after Phil for a few hours. Mick was still working on the lorries and going away for days at a time, but now he had total control, because we were dependent on him. He exercised that control by keeping Mum so short of money that there would be days when there was no food at all in the house, and we were always hungry.

The only way to survive was to steal food. Mum couldn't risk it: she'd have been up in court if she'd been caught and we'd have been taken into care. But I was underage, so it was unlikely I'd be prosecuted. She used to give me lists of things to steal from the supermarket, and I got away with it, which was a relief because it literally was the difference between starving and eating.

On one occasion I was doing well, collecting everything on Mum's list, plus a little present for baby Phil and some hairspray to cheer her up. I had pushed a packet of Lurpak butter into my back pocket. As I was slipping out through the entrance, however, one of the security guards stopped me and marched me to the manager's office. I put on a great act: I showed them the shopping list and said I'd lost Mum's £5 note on the way there. I cried, and they obviously believed me, because they said they would let me off, but of course I couldn't keep the shopping.

Just as I was leaving the office, the security man said, 'Have you got anything on you that belongs to this store?'

I shook my head, but then I remembered the Lurpak and realised I'd better come clean. I was worried that if I'd been searched and they'd found it, they'd send for the police. When I pulled it out, it was flattened and melting, as I'd been sitting on it for the past ten minutes. That day we went hungry.

On another occasion, though, I managed to steal some sausages and chops from a butcher's van, and Mum literally burst into tears of relief when she saw them. She was a kind, honest woman, and with Nan dead she had nobody to turn to.

I started at a new school, but I have absolutely no memory of it. Weirdly, I have no memory of abuse in Heswall either – probably because Mick was away a lot. What I do remember is the police turning the place over a couple of times looking for things: the CID were always on Mick's tail. His criminal friends also turned up there a few times. I can remember them all sitting round the table talking, drinking and smoking cigars.

Mum handed me a cigar and said, 'Take it to Mick and say, "Here's a cigar, Dad," and see what he does.'

I did as I was told. It was the first time I had ever called him 'Dad', and he gave me a big hug and beamed at me. I realised I had pleased him and I naïvely thought, Maybe if I always call him Dad, he'll like me more and he won't touch me.

I called him 'Dad' after that, but in my head I never thought of him as my father. Tom and I still used to refer to him as 'It', and Donna and I sometimes called him 'Mick the Prick', feeling very naughty for using a swear word, but our favourite name for him was still 'the Nutter'.

We were only in Heswall for a matter of weeks, not even months. All too soon we were on the move once more, and again there was no explanation. But this time we were heading right back into the centre of Liverpool.

CHAPTER FIVE

It was January 1971 and our new home was the Harvey Hotel, in Lime Street, not far from the railway station. Mum and Mick took over as managers, and we lived in two bedrooms on the first floor. Our bedroom had two single beds and Tom and I used to take turns to share with Phil. It wasn't a posh hotel – quite the opposite. It was a dosshouse where prostitutes rented rooms by the hour to service their clients ('Johns') who they picked up in the streets around the station.

It was hardly a suitable place for a young family, but Mum had no choice. It was a ramshackle old building, with steps up to the main door. In the hallway there was a counter, where we used to book in the customers, who stayed for an hour or two. One bedroom could be rented out four or five times in one night, and although I was only ten when we moved there, I was soon booking in the girls and their clients, and inspecting the rooms when they left. If the sheets were very stained, I had to change them – if not, it was just a matter of straightening them and emptying condoms from the bins.

There were two floors, each with five bedrooms and a bathroom. The rooms were very functional, with a couple of blankets and sheets in each, and a tea and coffee machine. On the ground floor there was a dining room, where Mum would make breakfast for anyone who stayed the night, and a living room, with a television, where we would sit. Sometimes the working girls would sit with us, drinking coffee before going back out on the streets again.

Tom and I had to help serve breakfast and do the washing up. We'd get tips from the prostitutes. Some of them disapproved of us working in the hotel: they didn't think it was right for children to be there, looking after a toddler and supervising the rough-looking clientele. But they were generous, and we usually ended up with some money for sweets.

Most of the hotels along the street were in the same trade as the Harvey, catering to prostitutes and their clients, with the odd normal guest, but the one immediately next door to ours was respectable and was run by an elderly woman who refused to deal with the girls who were on the game. She was lovely and would always give us a bar of chocolate or an apple when she saw us sitting on the steps of the Harvey. She wouldn't set foot in our hotel, and we scruffy little street urchins weren't really welcome in hers, but she was always kind to us.

For the next six months Tom and I didn't go to school. When our jobs at the hotel were done, we roamed the streets, hanging around Lime Street Station watching the trains or just wandering about the city centre. Looking back, it's a wonder we didn't get into more trouble than we did.

Mick started abusing me again as soon as we moved to the hotel. It was easier for him now because there were so many rooms where he could drag me for a quick feel. Because Mum was so busy and Tom was often out, he'd frequently just bark out his orders: 'Get on your knees and suck me off' or 'Wank me off.'

Beneath the Harvey Hotel, in the basement, was a club, which was nothing to do with the hotel. It opened in the afternoons, but was usually busy only in the evenings, when the music would be loud, and raucous groups of people would spill in and out.

One afternoon Tom and I were sitting on the steps of the

hotel wondering what to do with ourselves. The days dragged now that we didn't go to school. I noticed that the club door was open and I said, 'Let's go in and see if we can cadge a packet of crisps and a bottle of pop.' Occasionally the bar staff would give us crisps, so we thought it was worth a try. But when we got inside, the place was empty and the only lights that were on were those over the bar.

'Let's help ourselves to some crisps and scram,' Tom said.

Behind the bar was a large cardboard box, which said, 'Walkers crisps' on the side. I opened it, intending to nick a couple of packets. To our amazement, it was full of bags of coins, loads of them. We didn't think twice. I stuffed two bags inside each of my knee-length socks and another in my knickers. Tom filled his pockets, and then we ran for it. We escaped from the club and made our way to the back of the building, where there were some garages and a few corners where we could hide. We squatted on the cold ground and excitedly counted the money: it came to £20. It was riches beyond our dreams.

'We'll get battered,' I said.

'We get battered anyway,' said Tom.

We took about £6 of the money, put the rest back in the bags and stashed it in a secret hiding place. There was a small metal grille outside the hotel that gave access to a drain. When you lifted the cover, there was a shelf inside, above the drop to the water. We'd seen it before, when we'd opened the drain cover.

Then we walked to the station and phoned Donna from a callbox, telling her to bring her brothers into town to meet us. It must have been a school holiday because they were about. We had a great day. We played in the arcades, and then we all went to a café called the Punch and Judy, set into the side of a hill alongside the station, and bought hamburgers and chips and juice. We stuffed ourselves silly with sweets, then roamed around looking for something to do.

I'm not proud of what I did next, but considering the freedom we had it's remarkable that it's the worst thing that happened. We were in the St John's Precinct, on a bridge overlooking what today would be called a shopping centre. We had nicked two bottles of sauce from the Punch and Judy, one red and one brown. Looking down from the bridge, we saw a woman emerge from a hairdresser's below, her hair all backcombed and lacquered into a blonde bouffant. On impulse, I leaned over the bridge and squirted a huge dollop of tomato sauce, which landed on her head and ran down her face. She screamed and two security guards appeared. Spotting us, they took the steps to the bridge two at a time. I was determined we weren't going to be arrested, so I told the others to run and I pulled a large fire hydrant from the wall and turned it on them. A full blast of water hit them, and the power of it wrenched the hose from my hand. The security men were halted, and more concerned about stopping the water than catching us, so we got away. It was very naughty, I know, but it was also one of the most fun days of my childhood. When we got home, we expected a big fuss about the robbery from the club, but nothing was ever mentioned. We had a further three days out on the stolen money.

It was at the Harvey Hotel that I developed an obsessive hatred for washing myself. Perhaps it was because the earliest abuse had involved Mick washing me. More likely it was because I felt that if I was dirty and smelly, he wouldn't want to come near me. If I was clean, what he did to me would make me dirty anyway, so I might as well stay dirty. I stopped brushing my hair, cleaning my teeth and bathing. As Tom and I weren't in school, I didn't have to worry about what other children thought of my smelly state.

I also stopped Mick being involved in washing me by telling Mum I was old enough to take care of myself and didn't want to be washed by a man. When she told him, he was offended and said that I had to be watched to make sure I did it properly, but for once Mum dug her heels in: 'She's embarrassed. She's ten and is starting to bud in certain places – she's got to have some privacy from now on.'

I really admired her for standing up to him, and I thought, You don't know it, but you've just saved me. He can't use washing me as an excuse any more.

But he didn't need an excuse. Just before my eleventh birthday, when we had been at the Harvey Hotel for about two months, he and Mum went out in the evening, leaving me and Tom in charge of the hotel and of Phil. If any of the customers said anything about us being so young, we always told them our dad was busy in the back room. We were under strict instructions never to let anyone know we were there on our own, probably because of the risk of money being taken.

Mick and Mum went out a lot – he liked to socialise and enjoyed being so close to the city centre. On this occasion, Tom and I had spent the day mucking about around Lime Street Station during the day and had walked up to Lark Lane to hang out at our old school and see our friends. We'd come back home for our dinner and had then been given our instructions for the evening. We were to put Phil to bed at 7.30 p.m. and were to go to bed ourselves by 11 p.m., after locking the doors. Unusually, Mick had insisted that we all sleep in the double bed in the master bedroom, instead of sharing the two single beds in our room. I thought it strange, but could never have imagined what was to come.

We checked in three or four prostitutes that night, but I only had to change one lot of sheets. I can remember the evening clearly because it was the first time Tom saw a naked woman. He'd been peeping through the keyhole of one of the rooms and he came running up to me, shouting, 'Sharon, Sharon, you've got to look – they've got no clothes on.' He was falling about laughing. I had no intention of looking, because to me anything to do with sex was not funny, it was disgusting. The details of that evening are clearly etched in my memory. We could hear the music from the club downstairs. That night they were playing 'My Sweet Lord' by George Harrison over and over.

We did as we were told and all slept in Mum's bed, little Phil against the wall, Tom in the middle and me at the side. I don't know how long I had been asleep, but I woke to find Mick leaning over me. He pushed little Phil up nearer to the wall, shuffled Tom along, then me and climbed into the bed next to me.

I felt sick and was panicking. Where was Mum? I asked myself desperately. I was wide awake, but pretended to be asleep. He started kissing me and touching me, stroking my buttocks. He reeked of alcohol and stale sweat. I tried to turn away, but he grabbed my face and said in a loud whisper, 'Fucking look at me when I'm talking to you. I know you're awake, you little bitch.'

I opened my eyes and looked at him. He roughly manoeuvred me underneath him and pulled his body onto me. For the first time he was stripped naked and I was horrified by his chest hair, which was in my face. With one arm on the bed and the other covering my mouth, he raised himself above me and I suddenly felt a jolt of pain, like an electric shock passing through my whole body. Fear overwhelmed me, but I was powerless to fight back. Through living in the hotel and dealing with prostitutes I knew a little about sex, but I hadn't been prepared for what it actually involved. The sharpness subsided to a ripping sensation, but with only spit for lubrication the pain was intense. I could feel his thing thrusting into me brutally. Then there was a deep churning feeling in my stomach, as if something was reaching right up inside me and stirring up my insides. I tried to scream, but I couldn't breathe – he was covering my mouth and my nose. I panicked and struggled, and he moved his hand away from my nose but left it clamped down on my mouth. He kept on pumping up and down inside me. I thought it would never end. Eventually I passed out – whether through pain or shock I don't know.

When I woke up, it was morning and my brothers had gone from the bed. When I tried to move, I was in agony. It took a few seconds to sink in, to remember why I was in Mum's bedroom and what had happened to me. The pain was extreme; I felt as though I had been ripped apart. I sat up carefully, to avoid hurting myself, and glanced down. I was horrified to see there was blood on my legs and on the sheets. Large, angry purple bruises were blooming on my inner thighs.

I realised with a jolt that Mick was in the room, sitting at the dressing table. He had clean sheets in his hand and was looking at me in disgust. 'Look what you've done, you dirty little bitch,' he spat venomously. 'You've put blood on the bed.' He threw my clothes and a towel at me and told me to go and get myself washed and then go out to play.

I walked slowly and painfully across the room, with my bruised legs wide apart. I was too distressed to cry, even as the memories of the night before flooded back.

Just then he said very deliberately, enunciating every syllable, 'You say anything and you, your mother and your brothers, all dead.' He drew his hand across his throat. I had heard this threat many times before and genuinely believed that by submitting to him I was keeping my family safe. I felt like I was bargaining with the devil to keep his sordid secrets safe.

Then he handed me sixpence. I took it. I don't know why; I have often wished I had let it fall to the floor. By taking it I was accepting payment, which meant I was accepting him doing it.

Before I left the room, I asked where Mum was, and he told me they had a big fight and she had gone to stay with friends. I didn't believe him; I thought he had killed her. I was in turmoil. My mind was racing. She's dead. I'll never see her again, I told myself desperately.

Looking back, I can see that he had planned everything: he had known she wouldn't be coming home when he had told us all to go into his bed.

In the bathroom, I locked the door and braced myself to look at my legs. There was no fresh blood; it was dried on. I was relieved that I wasn't still bleeding – perhaps he hadn't done any permanent damage – but when I tried to pee, the awful searing pain of the night before shot through me again. As the wee trickled out, the burning sensation was so intense I had to grit my teeth to stop myself screaming. I knew, as I always did, that if I made any noise, it would be worse for me and he would punish me. The burning pain when I peed would continue for a few days.

I really was at my lowest ebb. I knew that what had happened to me was the 'shag' he had been promising me for the last few years: this was my fate. I now had another awful thing to dread, and I assumed it would hurt just as much each time as it had the first time.

I was desperately confused and distressed. From being very young, only five or six, he had told me regularly that all little girls did things with their daddies to make their daddies feel good, but that their mummies must never find out. 'When the mummies find out, the little girls go to live in children's homes and never see their mummies again,' he said. As I got older, I questioned it: I knew Donna never had to do the things I did; that's why I wished I could live in her family, not mine. But maybe some other girls did it. How was I to know? Maybe it was as normal as he tried to make out. All I could be certain of was that I hated it.

But the biggest worry, far overreaching the shock and confusion I felt about the rape, was my worry about Mum. She still hadn't returned home by late morning and I was worried sick about her. The next few hours passed in mounting fear but then, thank God, the phone rang and it was her. She told me that she was staying with her friends Doreen and Henry.

'Can't we come too?' I asked.

'No, because it's a two-bedroom place and Auntie Doreen has three children here anyway, so I'm sleeping on the couch. But I'll sort something out and come for you soon.'

I was so relieved to hear her voice that I didn't care that we were being left with Mick. Mum was alive, that was all that mattered. She spoke to Tom and Phil, and told them to be good boys.

Until about September we lived on our own with Mick Garvey in the hotel, and every day I prayed would be the day that Mum came for us. She met up with us two or three times a week, ringing us and telling us to meet her at the end of the road. She'd take us into town, buy us a burger and shower us with presents and treats. I could tell she felt really bad about leaving us, so I always tried to be cheerful when we saw her. Little Phil would cry and cling to her, and I could see how upset and worried she was, so I was determined not to burden her any more. We would so look forward to being with her, but the time seemed to pass very quickly.

Back at the hotel, I attempted to take on her role of looking after Tom and Phil, especially little Phil. I tried to make sure he was never left alone with Mick.

This was a truly terrible time in my life, without even the escape of school to rescue me. Tom and I were Mick's little slaves, helping run the hotel. He got a woman in to do the cooking and some of the cleaning, but we were expected to do everything else. His low-level criminality continued, and I once had to hide a gun under my mattress. Another time, he hid a couple of suitcases full of papers. CID officers continued to be regular visitors; they knew me and Tom by name. In the evenings he would sometimes have his cronies round to play cards. I was expected to serve them beer, and although I was just eleven, they'd leer at me and say things like, 'You're getting to be a big girl, Sharon. In a year or two I'll have trouble keeping my hands off you.' I hated it, and it made me even more determined to keep myself filthy and unattractive.

At night the boys were sent to bed earlier than me, and then he would take me into the kitchen and put the sneck on the door to prevent anyone coming in. He could do what he liked with me. I was at his mercy. He sat me on the edge of the kitchen table and raped me repeatedly. I used my survival techniques and prayed for Mum to rescue us, but a darkness was descending over me and I began to think I would never be free of him.

The best nights were the nights he brought other women home with him. I knew when I heard him rolling in drunk with some floozy that I wouldn't be raped that night. I think one of the reasons Mum never suspected he was a paedophile was because he always chased after anything in a skirt. She knew he was unfaithful with other women, so she never imagined he was into children.

The worst days were when he came back for seconds. He'd rape me during the day when Phil was asleep and Tom was out, and at first this would fill me with a sense of security – it was over – but then he'd do it again at night. During those few months without Mum I was raped maybe five or six times a week. If I managed to get to bed before he did it, he'd come into the room, pick up Phil and put him in bed with Tom, then force himself on me. I took to wearing three pairs of knickers, with pyjamas on top, and sleeping with the blanket wrapped tight round me. But he always found his way in.

Once or twice I scored a victory by suddenly making a noise and thrashing around as if I was having a bad dream. The boys would wake up and he'd hurriedly zip himself up and whisper to them, 'Shush, go back to sleep. I've just come in because Sharon's having a nightmare.'

The only person I told about the rapes was Donna, and again I spared her the details. She could sense when something truly terrible, worse than usual, was happening to me, and when I met up with her one day soon after the first rape, I burst into tears. It was all so shocking for me, and I felt unbearably alone.

'He put his dick in me,' was all I said. We knew what a dick was – it was the usual street name that all the kids used, and ever since they were tiny Mum had always used 'dicky' to Tom and Phil.

Seeing me so upset, Donna cried, too. We didn't talk about it any more. I never discussed the details, and she never asked. It was as if what was happening to me was too big for words. But it was always a great comfort to me that Donna knew. Although she couldn't share my pain, her quiet acceptance of me made me feel better. After we sobbed together for a few minutes, she said, 'We're sisters. Let's be real sisters.'

I didn't know what she meant.

'Let's do what the Indians do and cut ourselves and mix our blood. Then we'll be sisters for ever.'

We found a piece of broken beer bottle on the cobbled area

at the taxi entrance to the station, crouched against a wall, cut our fingers and held them together. Nobody took any notice of us, two little misfits, but for me it was a very important moment. It meant I had an ally, a friend, and felt a little less alone.

We saw Mum whenever we could, but she never came back to the hotel. We'd walk the couple of miles to Doreen's house, pushing Phil in the pram, or meet her in town. We'd constantly beg to live with her, and she'd have tears in her eyes when she promised us that we would all be together again soon.

When September came, we were enrolled in schools for the first time in nine months. Because I was now eleven, I went to secondary school, not far from the junior school Tom went to, where Phil was enrolled in the nursery. I didn't know anybody at this school. I was dirty and smelly and a bit overweight, so it was hard to make friends. Nevertheless I was relieved to be back in a classroom. I loved school – it was a refuge from the rest of my life. I had to wear a grey uniform and black shoes. I can remember Mum coming to meet me at the school with new shoes for me. I had permission to leave school ten minutes before the end of lessons, which gave me time to collect Tom and Phil and take them home.

None of us had time to settle into our new schools, because soon we were on the move again. This time, though, it was a wonderful move. One day as I left school Mum was there waiting for me with Tom and Phil. I was delighted to see her and ran over excitedly. She smilingly told us she had a new house for us all to live in together. My first and only question was 'Is he coming?'

When she said no, my happiness was complete. She had a taxi waiting, and she took us to a house in the Halewood area of Liverpool, which she had been given by the council. She had collected our clothes and toys from the hotel earlier in the day, taking Uncle Gordon and a friend of his with her in case Mick turned nasty. She told me he was OK about us leaving.

Now it was just her, me, Tom and Phil. I was happier than I had been since the day Mick Garvey had walked into my life.

CHAPTER SIX

Our ground-floor maisonette in Halewood was, to me, a palace. We didn't move in with much in the way of furniture or belongings, but there was one truly wonderful thing about our new home: no Mick Garvey. Life was sweet. Tom and I didn't have to work in the hotel any more, and I could sleep peacefully in my bed at night.

Mum told us it was a fresh start, and that's exactly how it felt. Just being able to walk home and into the house, sit down in front of the television, go to bed when I wanted and sleep as much as I liked – such normal things for most people – were great gifts, and I savoured them. I missed Donna, because we were a long way from Lark Lane, but she came to visit a couple of times.

It was a respectable area with good neighbours. Three doors away was a relative of Mum's (I think she was a cousin) with her husband and a clutch of teenage sons, and in the maisonette above us was a girl who went to the same school as me and became my best friend, apart from Donna. The maisonette had three bedrooms, so I had a room to myself, and there was a garden, and shops across the road. Ever the homemaker, Mum very quickly made it comfortable and homely. The music came back into our lives, and Mum seemed so much happier. She was healthy and refreshed from her months away from Mick. She'd put on some weight and was delighted to be back with her children. She started dating a

66

taxi driver called Tony, and he was a really lovely guy who made us all laugh.

By this time Uncle Gordon had married Anne, and they had a beautiful, big baby, also called Gordon. They came to see us, now that we were free of the monster. I remember them turning up in a taxi with little Gordon, and I instantly fell in love with this chunky little chap.

We had a lovely Christmas that year, 1971. Money was very scarce, but we were grateful for what we had. We were together and happy. Little Phil was still going to see his father, but the rest of us had nothing to do with him. We were finally rid of him and a whole new life without him stretched ahead of me.

Unfortunately, though, Mick Garvey was still able to exert his power over us. One Sunday he had access to Phil and had been supposed to return him in the afternoon, but by evening he wasn't back. Poor Mum was distraught, and even more shattered when the next day she received a message from Mick to say that he had taken Phil, who was not yet four years old, to live with him in America. How could he be so cruel?

I have no idea why or how Mick came to go to America. If Mum knew, she never told me. I don't even know which part of America he went to. I would have been glad Mick was thousands of miles away if only Phil had been safe at home with us.

It was an awful time. Mum was beside herself, but I was in an even worse state because I had the added worry that he might start abusing Phil. Looking back, this was perhaps one of the few occasions when I could have told Mum what had happened to me, but I was still afraid of him, and I thought that if Mum knew, he would kill her to stop her telling anyone. Also, it would double her fears and worries over Phil.

Mum tried everything to trace them in the States. She knew Mick had some relatives there, but when she contacted them, they had no news of him. In desperation she got in touch with his family here. We had met them a couple of times, but not often, because they lived in Luton. His father, Charlie, was an Irishman, a real gentleman, but Mum was suspicious of his mother, Frances, and always warned me not to tell her any of our business. Mick was the eldest of their children, followed by his brother, John, and a sister, Linda, who adored her eldest brother. It was John who came to our rescue. We didn't know him well. He was smaller than his brother and always domineered by him. I had thought of him as Mick Garvey's hanger-on, but he proved to me that he was much more than that and was a man of some integrity.

John had tracked his brother down in the States, and Mum somehow raised the money for him to fly out there. (I think she had to borrow it, because she couldn't have funded it from her part-time cleaning job.) She gave John a passport in Phil's name, and he flew out and literally snatched Phil, who he luckily found playing in the front garden of the place that Mick was renting. John whisked him into the car, then to the airport and back home to us.

The first I knew about the dramatic rescue was when I got in from school and Mum told me that Phil was on his way. We were all jubilant. When he arrived, we couldn't stop hugging and kissing him. Even though he had only been away for a few weeks, he seemed to have grown, and for the first few days he was very quiet.

Now that Phil was home, we could truly be happy. The idea that there was a whole ocean between us and Mick Garvey was a great comfort to me. I was sleeping better, not lying awake afraid of what might happen. Even so, years of abuse had inevitably left a savage mark on me. I still had my phobia about washing, and I always wore three pairs of knickers with tights over the top. On bad days, I'd even put more knickers on top of that. When I changed them, I'd hide them in my room or throw them away instead of washing them. It's clear to me now I was suffering from some sort of obsessive compulsive disorder. My mother tried to get a grip of my personal hygiene. When she found the unwashed knickers, she'd demand an explanation, but I had none to give. She would tell me I was a 'dirty, smelly cow'.

I was also developing an obsession with turning door handles and creaking floorboards. I couldn't stand having the bedroom door shut. I first realised there was a problem when I came home late from school one day and Mum was angry and sent me to my room. When she came up to go to the bathroom and saw me sitting on the bed, she was cross and said, 'Don't just sit there doing nothing – get on with your homework.' As she left, she slammed the door.

A few minutes later I saw the handle turning very slowly. I freaked, thinking it was Mick Garvey. In fact it was Tom, sneaking a biscuit up to me, but it made me realise I was terrified of door handles.

I also cried a lot, mostly involuntarily. I'd be walking along the street and burst into tears for no reason. I was constantly vomiting, and at school I spent a lot of time in the toilets being sick.

My periods started while we were living in Halewood. I was terrified as I had no idea what the blood was, at first thinking I must have sat on something that had gone inside me and cut me. When the bleeding didn't stop, I thought I was going to die. I wouldn't talk to anyone about that part of my body – it was the part I tried to deny existed.

Eventually Mum found some bloodstained knickers. 'Why didn't you tell me you'd come on your period?' she said, astonished.

It never occurred to her that nobody had told me what a period was. She gave me a hug and bought me sanitary pads. But I still had no sex education. I didn't know that periods were anything to do with babies, and that having sex made babies. I suppose most kids pick it all up in playground whispers, but I was in denial about anything to do with that side of life and would shut myself off from any conversations like that at school. In some ways I was experienced far beyond my age, but in others I was very young and naïve.

I was still writing my morbid poetry. One short poem I wrote at eleven went:

> *Tick, tock, tick, tock, tick, tock.*
> *Hear the clock ticking by.*
> *Tell me, please,*
> *When's my time to die?*

Again I was giving off lots of signals to show how disturbed I was, but nobody picked up on them. My school reports said I was a dreamer with a vivid imagination, in a world of my own. Nobody ever tried to find out what that world was or why I went there.

I believe that if we had stayed in Halewood, just the four of us, I could gradually have recovered from my obsessions, but my life was never that simple. Our happy time ended with a phone call. We didn't have a phone at home, so calls were made and received at a box a couple of streets away. One afternoon Mum told us to put our coats on and we walked round there. The phone rang and Mum answered. I couldn't hear the other half of the conversation, just Mum's responses: 'I want to, I do…I don't know. I'll have to ask the kids…You know I do…'

I thought something was going on, but I had no inkling of the terrible news that Mum was about to break. When we got home, she sat us down and said, 'It's up to you what we do, but I think we should do it. Mick's back and he wants us to go and live with him in Clacton. He's got a job there. We'd be living on the fairground, right on the beach, in a caravan.'

The words 'beach' and 'fairground' were all it took: the boys were jumping up and down with excitement, and Tom was singing, 'We're going to the beach, going to the fair, yeah, yeah, yeah!'

Mum said, 'What about you, Sharon?'

I said quite simply that I didn't want to go.

'We'll be at the beach. You can help out on the fairground,' she said coaxingly.

I turned my back and walked away: I knew we would go, whatever I wanted.

Mum seemed excited and happy to be going back to him. I couldn't understand it. I thought, He beats you and he drinks all the money, so how can it be good to go back to him? But I said nothing to her. I can see now that she was still in love with him, and always felt she could change him.

'It's a fresh start – he'll be different,' she promised. 'You'll all have such fun living by the sea.'

A little bit of me believed her. Perhaps it would be different. But deep down I felt a great weight settling on me again. Life had been, for a brief spell, really great. Now it was back to normal, back to living in fear.

But there was worse to come. Mum and Phil went, and left me and Tom behind.

'I'm just going to make sure he's changed, and check that we've got somewhere nice to live,' she said, when she explained that we would be staying with her relatives up the road for a short time. At first I was pleased – the last thing I wanted was to go and see Mick Garvey – but I didn't settle in our new lodgings. I was terrified that the man of the house would rape me, and that his teenage sons might too. I feel ashamed, looking back, that I could think so badly of good people, but it was all I knew.

The first thing that happened was that the woman said she

would run a nice hot bath for me – I really was a stinky little thing – but I panicked, thinking that when I got my clothes off, someone would come in and abuse me. Although the door to the bathroom was frosted glass, I hung a towel over it, and then sat rigid in the bath, waiting for the worst.

For three nights I didn't sleep at all. I forced myself to stay awake. It was something I always did with Mick Garvey, because the abuse had always seemed worse if I'd been deeply asleep and dreaming when it started. But after three sleepless nights my eyes were red and bloodshot and I was falling asleep at school. The school rang up the woman, but she couldn't understand it: she was sending me to bed at 8 p.m. Things got slightly easier when I did relax enough to sleep, but then one night I had the most horrendous nightmare. I dreamed that Mick Garvey had killed Mum so that he could have Phil to himself. I thought he had murdered her, buried her at Clacton, then gone to the US again and nobody would ever find him. I started screaming in the night, and I was being difficult in other ways: stealing packets of biscuits and other bits and pieces. In the end, the family couldn't cope with me any longer. Tom was fine. He simply said, 'She'll be back – Mum won't let us down.' He was happy living with Mum's relatives; I was the only problem.

So I moved into the maisonette above our old one, with the girl who was at school with me and her family. I was better there, but I began wetting the bed. Everyone decided that it was because I was missing Mum, but really it was the stress of not knowing whether she was alive or dead, or if Mick was beating her up.

In the end, after a couple of months, Uncle Gordon and Auntie Anne rang Mum and told her that it was wrong to leave us there and that we were suffering. Gordon persuaded her that we should join the family in Clacton. He and Anne picked us up, with all our belongings, when we got home from school. He told the people I was living with that he was taking us home with him for the night, and the next day would drive us to Clacton. I had no time to say goodbye to any of my friends from school, but I was really glad to be going back to Mum, because I knew she must be alive if Gordon had spoken to her.

As soon as we left, Gordon said, 'You're going on a big adventure. I didn't want to tell you in front of those others, but I'm not taking you to your mum – we're putting you on a bus. Will you be OK?'

"Course we will,' I said confidently.

'But you'll have to change buses in London.'

That made it sound even more exciting, and Tom and I hugged each other in glee.

'London – that's where all the rich people live,' Tom said.

Gordon and Anne took us to the bus station in the centre of Liverpool and put us on a 10 p.m. coach for London. He was clearly worried about it and asked us several times, 'Are you sure you'll be OK?' We nodded resolutely.

He and Anne gave us sandwiches and bottles of pop. The arrangement was that Tom and I, aged ten and twelve, were to transfer at Victoria Coach Station in London to another bus for Clacton in the early hours of the morning, and Mum would meet us when we got there. I can remember Gordon's anxious face, watching us as the coach pulled out.

He and Anne drove behind our coach until we got to the motorway, and we sat on the back seat waving to them and blowing kisses. I realised how worried they were when I saw tears streaming down their cheeks. Gordon says he is still haunted by the guilt of putting two young children on a night coach on their own and can hardly believe he did it. But he was still only a teenager himself, with a wife and baby to care for.

Luckily, it all went OK. I don't remember much about the

journey to London because I think we both slept, although I tried to stay awake in case we missed the stop. As we pulled into the centre of London in the early hours of the morning, we were astonished to see people coming out of brightly lit clubs, some wearing evening dress, dicky bows and long gowns. We really did believe that London was full of millionaires. And when we had to wait for the Clacton bus, Tom said excitedly, 'Let's go and explore London.'

But I was worried about missing the Clacton bus, and we'd been told by Uncle Gordon not to go anywhere, so I said firmly, 'No, we're staying here.'

We sat on our cases for what seemed like a very long time, probably a couple of hours, until the bus arrived. There were few people about, and no cafés to get a cup of tea – not that we had any money.

When we reached Clacton-on-Sea, it was mid-morning, and we climbed off the coach expecting to see Mum. The pavement was very crowded with people getting off and on, but as the bus pulled away and the crowd cleared, we realised we were on our own. Mum was not there. Before I had time to think what to do, a car pulled up and a black man opened the window and shouted, 'Are youse waiting for your mum?'

When we said yes, he told us to hop in. He said he had been sent to pick us up. Unquestioningly, we hauled our big suitcases into the boot and climbed in. I shiver when I look back at how naïve we were, and how lucky – he really had been sent by Mum. We set off, driving through the thrilling sights of funfairs with big wheels, miles of arcades and sandy beaches, all busy because it was the start of the summer season. Then we left the town behind, passing through the countryside to the small coastal holiday town of St Osyth, five miles east of Clacton. We pulled into the Seawick Holiday Village, and the car stopped outside a small caravan.

I was relieved to see Mum waiting for us, smiling and very definitely alive. It was only when I hugged her that I really believed she was safe. I stayed close to her that whole first day, even though Tom and Phil were soon off playing. My joy at seeing her was so great that it even eclipsed the horror of seeing Mick Garvey again.

When he appeared, he just said gruffly, 'Hello, you two. I didn't think you'd get here.'

He was still a big brute of a man and still terrified me, but nothing could dampen my relief and happiness that Mum was alive, well and unharmed.

We stayed in the caravan for a week and then moved to a bigger chalet. It was still tiny and cramped compared to a house. There were two bedrooms, one for him and Mum and one for us kids, but the walls between them were like paper and you could hear the people in the next room breathing. For me that was a glorious reprieve: Mick didn't abuse me the whole time we were there, which was about five months. In fact, he didn't do anything to me, never even groped me or said anything dirty. I did my best to keep out of his way. Maybe he was trying to behave better, or maybe it simply was an impossible situation, with all of us living so much on top of each other. Whatever the reason, my fears began to subside and I hoped, like Mum did, that he really had changed.

He and Mum worked for Billy Ball, a jovial man who ran a big amusement arcade. Mum worked on the change counter most of the time, and Mick was a bingo caller and doorman. Tom was in his element, running wild, and I'd sometimes join him, with little Phil in tow. We missed the last four weeks of the summer term at school and couldn't believe our luck.

We had only been on holiday once in our lives, and that had been when Nan and Mum had taken us to Tenby for a week in a caravan. Their friend Paul, the barber in Lark Lane, drove us all the way, with our suitcases, in his tiny Mini. He came back for us at the end of the week; he is a really good man. We'd loved Tenby (I have a vivid memory of Tom swinging on a cow's tail), but it was tame compared to Clacton. Apart from that we'd only ever been on coach trips to see the lights at Blackpool, driving through once a year and never even getting off the coach. For me, the sea was the murky grey water of Liverpool docks. So Clacton and St Osyth were a real culture shock. Even the beaches seemed vast, and Tom and I felt we had landed in paradise. Phil was in his element too, loving the sand and the sea. One of my main jobs was to look after him and the children of various other people who worked there. Russ Abbot, who later became very famous as a comedian, was appearing there for the summer season with his band, the Black Abbots, and I used to babysit his children. He and his wife were living in a chalet not far from ours and were friendly with Mum and Mick.

My other big job was to keep the chalet clean and do the dishes. One day I was so sick of it that I simply emptied all the dirty dishes and the mess into a bin bag and dumped it outside, then cleaned and polished the chalet until it was spotless. Mum was delighted when she came in – until it was time to make the tea and there were no pans or plates. She really laid into me with her tongue.

At other times I had to help Mum at the change booth in Billy Ball's Arcades. If she went to fix one of the machines, I'd be left in charge of giving the holidaymakers the coins they needed to feed the hungry machines. Off duty, I made friends, but they were girls who came with their families for a week or, at best, two, so I never got close to anyone. Having said that, I did learn a lot from one group of girls I befriended.

We were all in the toilets at the clubhouse when one of them said, 'My sister lost her virginity last night.'

'Why don't we go and look for it?' I said, with no clue as to how dumb I sounded.

The other girls started laughing.

'Where's she lost it?' I persisted.

'It's her virginity.'

When I looked perplexed, they took pity on me.

'You know, when you first have sex.'

I didn't really know what they meant by 'have sex', but I knew it was connected to what Mick Garvey had done to me. I may have been twelve years old, but I was young and naïve for my age, despite what had happened to me. I hadn't done any of the normal things girls do, like going to discos or youth clubs. Since we'd moved away from Donna, I hadn't had any friends close enough to talk to about intimate things, and I had never been at the same school long enough to establish a group of friends.

Hearing that other people had this thing called sex made me feel sick. I thought, the Nutter's right. It's not just him; it's everyone.

'Before you have sex you're a virgin,' my young teacher carried on matter-of-factly, 'and afterwards you're not no more, so you've lost your virginity.'

My mind was racing. I never had one, I thought. I never had one of these virginity things. He took that, as well as everything else. I never had what these girls have got, so that they can lose it.

Realising I knew nothing, the girls went on to give me a full sex lesson, telling me where babies came from.

'When someone puts their dicky dong inside you, that's how you get babies unless you take precautions and use johnnies.'

I listened wide-eyed with astonishment. I knew that the prostitutes at the Harvey Hotel had used condoms, but I'd had no idea why – I'd always thought it was something to do with hygiene. Once birth control had been explained, I was even more worried and confused. After I'd left the girls, I started to panic: If that's what makes babies, will I have one if he comes near me again?

Another incident from our time by the seaside is seared into my memory. We had all gone to the beach for the day, Mick, Mum, Mum's friends Joycie and Alfie, and a gaggle of us kids. We had a blow-up rubber dinghy, and I paddled out to sea on it, bobbing along happily in the sunshine with my eyes closed. Suddenly my dreams were shattered by a voice shouting, 'Help! My baby, my baby!' Startled, I opened my eyes and looked around. The beach looked small and far away, but close to me was a rowing boat with a family in it: a man, woman and three children. They were standing up and shouting as the boat slowly sank. At first I confess I laughed, because it looked like something out of a comic film, but I soon realised they were in genuine trouble. I paddled across and by the time I got there they were all in the water. I told the mother and father to hold on to my dinghy while I got the children. I'm not much of a swimmer, but I managed to get the three children back to my dinghy. The mother was still screaming 'My baby!' and I thought there must be a baby below the waves. I had to summon all my courage to dive down looking for the baby, and I went three times altogether. It was only when, after my third dive, I paused to get my breath that I saw the mother hugging the youngest of the three kids, a girl, and exclaiming, 'My baby, my baby!' Thank God there wasn't a drowned baby – it was just her name for her youngest. (For years Mum, Tom and I called Phil 'the baby', much to his annoyance when he was a big kid.)

The father climbed into the dinghy and pulled the youngest child in with him. The other two, the mother and me clung to the side and I told them all to kick their legs as we slowly made for the beach. It turned out that none of them could swim. We came to the shore, where a crowd of people had gathered, and the family were soon whisked away, with a big fuss being made of them. I picked up the dinghy and walked back to the other side of the beach, where our picnic party was sitting.

'Mum, guess what? I've just saved some people's lives, a whole family.'

Mum jumped up off her towel and, in front of everyone, gave me a good slap. 'You're lying again. Get in the car.' She frogmarched me to the car park, threw me in and drove me back to the chalet, where she gave me a good hiding. 'You lying little cow,' she shrieked. 'Telling lies when people could really be drowning. You stay here for the rest of the day.'

It hurt really badly. The physical pain of the beating wasn't bad – I had endured far, far worse from Mick Garvey – but from Mum it hurt me much more because she so rarely did it. But the biggest hurt of all was the realisation that Mick had so successfully turned me into a liar in Mum's eyes that nothing I ever said would be believed. I curled into a ball and cried myself to sleep.

When I woke a few hours later, the light was on. Mum came into the bedroom and wrapped her arms round me. 'Sharon, I'm so, so sorry,' she said, full of remorse.

Apparently her friend Joycie had walked across to the other side of the beach and had been there when the rescue took place. She met a friend and stayed there for a couple of hours, eventually strolling back and saying to Mum, 'Your Sharon's a right little heroine. She's only saved a whole family. None of them could swim. If she hadn't been there with her dinghy, they might all have drowned.'

Mum apologised profusely, but for me the damage was done. I knew now I could never tell her about the abuse; like he'd always told me, I would never be believed.

October came and the summer season tailed away to nothing. There is no sight sadder than a summer holiday village when the arcades are closed down, the shops and supermarkets are shuttered and closed, and the beach is deserted. We stayed until the very end, as Billy Ball's Arcades were the last to call it a day.

One morning I got up to find Mum and Mick loading all our possessions into the car. Everything we owned was being stashed in the boot and in the footwells in front of the back seat; we children would have to travel with our feet up. As usual, we weren't told where we were going. It took a while to pack, and by the time we set off it was late afternoon. We cuddled up together and fell asleep. When I woke, it was dark. The car was parked, and Mum and Mick weren't there. I had no clue where we were.

Shortly afterwards they returned. We drove for about five minutes and then stopped again, outside a boarded-up house. Mick went up to the door and with brute strength pulled off the wood that was nailed across it. He kicked open the door and we walked in. There was no electricity, and there were no floorboards in the hall.

Welcome to London. Welcome to our new home.

CHAPTER SEVEN

It was the middle of the night when we broke into the property in Knapp Road, Bow, East London. We had to balance on floor beams in the hall to get inside, but luckily Mick and Mum had torches. I don't know how they found it, but I heard them talking about someone who worked for the council, so I guess the place they stopped at first was where they were given (or paid for) the address of an abandoned property.

The house had once been a wool shop, and there was a boarded-up shop window in one of the derelict downstairs rooms. On that first night we three children slept on an old couch that had been left in the living room, wrapped in quilts that we brought in from the car. When I woke up, I went to the window and looked out. It was such a change from Clacton; all I could see were concrete blocks of maisonettes. I prayed that we were only going to be there for a couple of days.

Unfortunately, we were staying. My mum was magic with homes. The property was scheduled for eventual demolition, but she could make something from nothing, and had to many times in her life with Mick Garvey. It was the same with food: she could rustle up a good meal from anything. Within two to three weeks that house was lovely. Mick put floorboards in the hall, and Mum got busy with wallpaper and paint, and bought throws to cover the old couch. Nan's brass ornaments came out. Mum cleaned and scrubbed and polished; the smell of Pledge furniture polish is the most evocative smell I know and instantly brings my mother to mind. A van arrived and delivered some beds.

Mick Garvey solved the electricity problem by wiring the house up to an electricity pylon that was conveniently right outside. It more or less worked, but the kitchen was 'live' – we always had to wear our rubber-soled school plimsolls or we'd get small shocks through our feet, and all cooking had to be done with wooden spoons. We were banned from touching the cooker or the sink. I can remember once coming in and Mum telling me to stir the mince. Without thinking, I picked up a metal spoon and put it into the pan – the shock threw me across the room and my fingertips, under my nails, turned blue. On another occasion Mum collapsed on the floor from a shock. Little Phil was always forgetting to put his rubber shoes on and would run across the floor as if he was dancing through a fire. But, as Mick kept reminding us, at least the electricity was free.

I realised we were staying there when, in the first week, Mum took us to enrol in schools. Tom and Phil had a school very near to Knapp Road, but mine, Langdon Park School, was a twenty-minute walk away, close to Chrisp Street Market. I was very worried, starting back at school. We'd had five months off, and education had gone completely out of my head. Not only was this a new school, but I was joining the second year, and I was starting in November, a couple of months into the term. I was certain I would never make any friends. I rationalised it to myself, I don't want to make friends, because he'll do something wrong and we'll have to move again.

The new uniform was navy blue, but to my horror Mick and Mum said they were going to send me in my old grey uniform, to save money. I didn't want to draw attention to myself by being the only one in grey. Luckily, though, I'd grown so much in the summer months that it no longer fit me and I had to have a new uniform anyway.

On my first day I was sat next to the most gorgeous-looking girl I had ever seen. Her name was Madeleine Muscat. Even her name was the most beautiful thing I had ever heard. I was in complete awe of her long blonde hair, her blue eyes and her face, which to me looked rich and aristocratic because of her high cheekbones and Roman nose.

To my surprise, she was really friendly, and she became my best friend throughout secondary school. I envied her so much. Her parents had split up, so she lived with her mother and brother. To me, that was perfect: a house with no adult man in it. Madeleine's home was spotless, and when you went in, her mum would have biscuits and juice waiting for you, and there would be Irish music playing. Sometimes Madeleine would be stroppy with her mother – just normal teenage stuff – and I'd get really annoyed. Doesn't she know how lucky she is? I would wonder to myself.

I never told her anything about my real problems with Mick, but she knew I was afraid of him and couldn't take her back to our house as I never knew when he would be there. I was worried that if he saw my beautiful friend, he might try it on with her. But I also didn't want to draw attention to my friends, because I knew he would try to isolate me from them. Tom and Phil brought friends home, but life was still a lot more difficult for me than it was for them.

Mum met Madeleine and really liked her. She used to say, 'Why can't you be more like Madeleine? Why do you always have to cause fights?'

As for me, I was a complete contrast to look at. I was still dirty, refusing to wash or clean my teeth, and would only give my scraggy brown hair a cursory brush. I was always being told I looked miserable, which would annoy me. And the more they said it, the more miserable I became.

I was bullied and picked on. The older girls called me

names: 'Scruffy Squat Liver', 'Tramp', 'Squatter', 'Gravy Stain' (derived from my name, Garvey) and 'Dirty Scouser'. I've always been proud of my Liverpool accent, but at school it singled me out as a target, and I heard every joke about thieving Scousers that's ever been invented. My accent also seemed to rile Mick Garvey: 'You're in London now, girl, talk properly.' As far as I was concerned, whatever he'd taken from me, he wasn't having my accent and my Liverpool heritage. Phil was young enough to adopt a London accent easily, and Tom's slipped away more readily than mine, although it's still definitely there. I defiantly hung on to mine, and I will until I die.

Looking back, I can see that I stayed dirty as a way of keeping the pressure off. If I was a dirty little squatter, I didn't have to be anyone else; I could keep reality at bay. I had a belief that if I looked dirty and unattractive, Mick would leave me alone. Every morning I said to myself, Just get through today, just get through today.

I'd had almost a year's break from the abuse, all the time Mick and Mum were apart, and then for the past five months at Clacton. I dared to think that it was over. But of course it wasn't, and shortly after moving to London it started again, as bad as ever. Worse, in many ways, because now I was old enough to understand the full horror of what was happening.

I had my own bedroom at Knapp Road, and in the beginning it was my little haven. There was a built-in wardrobe, a bed of my own, and although there were no carpets, I had a pretty blue rug with fringes at each end next to the bed. From the window I could see across the kitchen roof to the yard at the back. I asked if I could have a lock on my door, but Mick was quick to scotch that plan: 'That's not the way you live family life, with locks on doors. Besides, if there was a fire, she'd be locked in. It's dangerous. It would be like a prison,' he told Mum.

For me, a lock would have been the opposite of imprisonment: it would have been freedom from fear.

Mick started lorry-driving again, and Mum found work cleaning and catering. She made a really good friend, a wonderful woman called Eileen Rosser, and together they worked as silver-service waitresses and then set up their own small catering company, providing buffet food for corporate lunches and parties. My mum was a miracle worker: in that live kitchen she cooked trays full of food, packed it all in boxes and covered it with tinfoil.

We didn't pay rent or electricity bills, so there seemed to be a bit more money, and every Saturday Mum would take us to the market, where we'd have pie and mash or a chippie meal. She always bought us things: clothes for me, toys for the boys. She was very generous when she had money.

One evening Mum and Eileen were out doing the catering for a wedding reception, and Tom was staying over with a friend from school. He always found it easy to make friends and, like me, tried to keep out of Mick's way as much as possible. Mick put Phil to bed and came downstairs to the living room where I was watching TV. He walked in, drew the curtains and said bluntly, 'Strip off.'

When he said those two words, my brain screamed in silent anguish. Oh, God, please don't let it be happening again. I turned to him in disbelief. It was a real shock. I'd been lulled into a false sense of security. I'd begun to believe we really were a proper family. All the time at Clacton he'd kept away from me, and for the very first time he had been treating me and Tom as equals with Phil – if Phil got an ice cream, we did too. He was still angry and violent with Mum, and I would have been a lot happier if we could go back to being just her and us kids, but for her sake I was making the best of it.

I could feel my heart pounding in my ears. I knew I was

trapped, and I was desolate, but also angry. In the year since he had last abused me I had grown up so much, and I now knew about the risk of pregnancy. I was determined he was not going to abuse me ever again.

Resolutely, I pulled my arms tight round me and said, 'No.'

It was the first time I had ever defied him, and I don't know where the courage came from, but the word just came out.

'What did you say to me?' he asked slowly and deliberately.

'No.'

'Don't give me any of your fucking backchat,' he hissed. He lowered his face to within an or inch or two of mine. I could smell his breath and pulled back. 'If I tell you to do something, you fucking do it. Now take your fucking clothes off.'

In despair, I started crying, but he ignored me and began to wrench my clothes off. I struggled, and he punched me, very hard, in the back of my head, twice.

'You will do as you are fucking told or I will fucking knock you out and do it anyway.' He then roughly stripped me and dragged me on to the couch, kneeling between my legs and performing oral sex.

It was awful, and to this day I have never been able to get rid of my feeling of disgust for it. In later life, in loving relationships, I have wanted to enjoy it, but I have never been able to get beyond the picture in my mind of his big ginger head between my legs. Yet again he has taken something from me: a part of my sexuality.

Afterwards he lay me on the floor with a cushion under my bottom and raped me. I tried to stop him, but he held both my hands above my head with one of his, to stop me struggling. I soon gave up the fight – it was completely futile and only hurt more if I struggled – and went back into the safety of my own head, watching the soil piling up in the grave around me.

Get it over with. Get it over with, I repeated to myself like a mantra.

When he had finished, he said, 'Go up to bed. Don't forget to fold your uniform properly.'

I did as I was told and lay shivering in bed, wondering how I would cope with the realisation that this was now my fate. This rape changed everything for me. All the time in Clacton I had allowed myself to feel that, perhaps, I could be normal. That was all I wanted; it wasn't a very big ambition. But now he had ripped even that away from me. I was too tired and upset to even cry. I just lay there feeling as if I was being crushed by a terrible weight. He'd taken my childhood; now he was taking my adolescence. There was no escape from him.

I couldn't tell Mum. She would only want to know why I hadn't said anything earlier. Besides, I still believed he would kill her, and Tom and Phil. I had no choice, but I expressed my turmoil in other ways. I became difficult, rebellious, hard to handle. I sulked and gave cheek. I began staying out late and making sure I was out of the house as much as possible. I played truant from school (although I always went in for my favourite English, art and history lessons).

Christmas came just a few weeks later, and it was both Heaven and Hell. We got lovely presents, because there was more money about, and we had a big tree, covered with lights, in the window. The house was filled with the smells of Mum's cakes and pies. But at the back of my mind I knew that with any opportunity he had, he would abuse me.

My body was growing up; I had breasts and body hair. I fell in love for the first time, which was very confusing for me, because I began to have pleasurable sexual feelings when I thought about Frankie Downer, the god on a motorbike who became the object of all my yearnings. I was shocked that I could feel like this about anyone.

One of the hardest things to come to terms with in my adult life has been that, like other abused children, I had sometimes felt pleasure when Mick was molesting me. I hadn't enjoyed it, but on a purely physical level if, in those early days when he simply fingered me, he hit upon a pleasurable movement, I couldn't prevent my body experiencing it. My body liked it, but I, Sharon, hated it. It is another reason why throughout my years of abuse I kept my body so separate from my mind and brain. Latterly, when he was brutally raping me, all feelings of pleasure disappeared, but I still lived with the guilt, blaming myself for being abused because perhaps at times I looked as if I enjoyed it, even though it was abhorrent to me.

Now I was experiencing those same tingles in my nerve endings for Frankie. The first time I saw him, I fell head over heels. I adored him with a vengeance. I was a dirty little twelve-year-old, and he was about sixteen, with long blond hair and blue eyes, which I remember describing in one of my poems as 'pools of blue water'. He would sit on the wall around the block of maisonettes opposite our house, talking with his mates, a typical gang of lads on a corner. I used to pretend to have to go to the shops, just to walk past them. Frankie soon spoke to me because at one time his family had lived in the house we were squatting in: they'd been rehoused when the property had been condemned and scheduled for demolition. It turned out that my bedroom had been his, which heightened my desire for him. I felt it was Fate linking us, and that one day he would come and take me away from all my problems, riding off into the sunset on the back of his bike.

He *did* let me ride on his bike. He'd give me his spare helmet and we'd zoom off – once, he took me at a hundred miles an hour around the Isle of Dogs. I'm sure he liked me, but he treated me like a princess, not a woman. Only once did he let his defences down, when we were sitting on the concrete steps inside one of the blocks of maisonettes, talking, and he put his arm round me and kissed me.

I melted and said, 'I love you, Frankie.'

He said, 'Don't be saying things like that. You're too young to love me. When you are older, you can love me.'

I was annoyed that he thought I was too young. Inside my head I was screaming, It's all right – you can have sex with me. I've done it already. My dad does it, so why don't you?

But although I think he was fond of me, he certainly wasn't going to get involved with a twelve-year-old. I hung around Frankie for about a year, taking great care not to let Mum or Mick know of my feelings for him. Then he found himself a girlfriend of his own age and disappeared off the face of my earth.

Falling in love with Frankie made me a little bit more careful about my personal hygiene. I washed my face, brushed my hair, put it up in a ponytail and cleaned my teeth. But I still had issues with my body. I could keep my face clean, but I didn't want to wash anywhere else. I was developing into a woman, which I hated; to me, growing up was associated with having sex, despite the fact the abuse had been happening to me since I was four years old. I was in complete conflict, disgusted with my own body, denying that I was becoming a woman, yet at the same time experiencing normal teenage yearnings for Frankie.

We had some sex education lessons at school, which cleared up everything about where babies came from, but also made me even more worried when Mick raped me. We were taught about sexually transmitted diseases, which put the fear of God into me. While the rest of the class giggled, I was frightened. From then on every cramp I felt made me convinced I had chlamydia or some other nasty disease.

Meanwhile, the rapes continued at home. Nothing else going on in my life made any difference to what happened to me behind closed doors. I had never had a choice in it, everything was dictated by Mick Garvey, and I was forced to do whatever he wanted.

He noticed I was taking more pride in my appearance and going out more, and he did his best to put a stop to it. He would say to Mum, 'She's slagging about, that little bitch.'

I'd try to get out when he wasn't aware of me going, but if he saw me I'd say, 'I'm only outside the door. I'm just waiting for Madeleine – she's walking down.'

'You're going nowhere, you slag,' he'd growl.

Sometimes he'd tell Mum he was taking me with him on his lorry to help with his delivery. He had a bunk behind the front seat and he'd rape me in there. He'd just park up anywhere, at the side of a busy road even, and draw the curtains.

Once again I was treading on eggshells, trying to anticipate when he would be home and when he would be away. Often he was away overnight, and occasionally he had to deliver something abroad, which was great because I got a few days off.

My survival strategies changed as I grew older. The circle I had built round me as a child was now a fog, which descended as soon as I got near home. If I could see the lorry from the bottom of Knapp Road, the fog became dense, but if the lorry was not there, it lifted partially and became a mist. I couldn't release it until I was inside the house and certain that he wasn't home, because sometimes he didn't have the lorry with him. Those were the cruellest of days – when I thought he wasn't home but would walk in to find him standing in the kitchen leering at me.

If he was there and he and Mum were arguing, the fog

became black and impenetrable. This was a time of a lot of violence and aggression, and poor Mum didn't know how to deal with it. When he was beating her up, she would call out to me – it was always me because I was the oldest.

'Sharon, get the police,' she'd plead as the blows rained down on her.

I would run to the phone box two hundred yards away and dial 999. 'My mum's getting beaten up by my stepdad,' I'd blurt out, panicked. 'He's killing her.'

Then I would go to the flats opposite our house and hide behind the wall. The police would turn up, and he'd open the door and talk to them. A couple of minutes later Mum would be by his side, a big smile on her face. Mick didn't care about where he hit her – I can remember her once talking to a policeman with blood pouring from her nose – because as long as she wasn't making a complaint, the police did nothing. They classed it as a 'domestic' in those days and didn't interfere. I would then be terrified of going home. I had thought the police were going to take him away, but now I knew I would get a good hiding for calling them.

It happened a lot, and at times I would think, Shall I call them? I'll only get battered. But if I don't call them, he might kill her.

I'd delay until her screaming was so bad that I couldn't stand it, and then I'd run to the callbox, knowing that I would, in all likelihood, end up with a beating.

She should be saving me, not me saving her. But if she saves me, he'll kill her, my mind would scream.

I was so confused, and it felt unfair that all the decisions seemed to be put on me. I didn't know whether I was an adult or a child. Can nobody see what's going on and rescue me? I asked myself in desperation.

*

One day, when I was thirteen, I came in from school and Mum was busy in the kitchen, chopping cabbage and peeling potatoes at the sink. I was chatting to her about my day when Mick came in.

'I've got a bone to pick with you,' he said.

I thought he was talking to Mum, but when I didn't respond, he prodded me in the back and said, 'You.'

'Me? Why?'

'Your room is a fucking disgrace,' he spat venomously.

'It's not that bad, Mick,' Mum said, trying to placate him.

'Yes it is. Get up them stairs. I'll give you five minutes to get your uniform off...' He paused, and for a bleak second I thought, Mum must know what he does to me, but he carried on '...and get something casual on. I'll be up to sit there while you tidy your room and do your homework.'

I looked at Mum and said, 'Mum, I'll do it when I come back in for tea.'

'Sharon, don't cause arguments, just do as your dad says,' she said wearily.

I went upstairs and put my tightest jeans on. I thought he would have to struggle to get inside them. Then I sat down and started my schoolwork.

He entered the room, came up behind me and dragged me to my feet by my neck. 'Get the fucking jeans off.'

'No.'

'Get the fucking jeans off *now*,' he roared.

'No, I'm going to tell Mum,' I said defiantly.

'Tell your mum and I'll stab her. I'm telling you now if she looks at me sideways just once, I'll stab her in the chest right in front of you. Do you want that?'

Once again I reluctantly did as I was told. The true horror for me was that he didn't want to rape me on the bed, but made me lie on the rug on the floor. Right below me, only a floorboard away, was my mum, making dinner.

Please hear me, Mum, I prayed. Please, God, make her come upstairs and catch him.

I longed for her to find out, to understand, to comfort me. Usually when he raped me, Mum wasn't in the house or was fast asleep. Doing it so openly, with her so close, was a terrible twist. That was his kick, part of his need for control. He wanted me to be that close to her, yet still helpless. It was his sadistic way of letting me know how much power he had. It was as if he was defying her to find out. To me, that meant only one thing: he really would kill her if she did catch him. I was haunted by the image of him stabbing her. I'd already seen her lying crumpled and broken on the floor after a savage beating, so it was no stretch of the imagination to see her fatally stabbed. I could picture the blood. While part of me cried out for her to come upstairs and help me, another part was terrified of the consequences if she did.

In desperation I struggled, but he hit me hard across my face with the back of his fist. It was a dismissive, back-handed swipe, as if I was nothing, just a piece of dirt, but it was hard and hurt. My teeth and jaw ached for hours afterwards. It worked: I stopped struggling and allowed him to do what he wanted. In many ways this rape was no worse than the others, and less violent than some, but for me, psychologically, it felt worse.

When it was over, he left me on the floor and didn't even tell me to tidy my room. I lay there, trying to shut it all out of my mind. Think about the essay you have to write, I told myself. What did the teacher say? I was now too old for daisy chains, but I was still compartmentalising things, shutting out what had been done to me.

Mick knew I was older, more mature, and he seemed to be increasingly worried about the risk of me telling someone. When he had me alone, he stepped up the threats: 'You haven't told anyone at school, have you? If you do, imagine your worst nightmare and then treble it. That's what's going to happen.'

I did feel a stronger urge to talk about it to others than I had when I was little. Once, in the girls' toilets, I let something out without thinking. Some older girls were hanging around in there smoking, and I had been using the toilet. One of them was telling the others about having sex with her boyfriend, obviously a first among this group.

'You didn't!'

'Yeah, we did.'

'What was it like?'

'Bloody fantastic!'

Spontaneously I said, 'What'll your dad do if he finds out?'

'He'll kill me,' she said.

'Yeah, because you're not supposed to have sex with anyone but your dad, are you?'

They all turned to look at me, and I'll never forget the look of shock and disgust on their faces. It was yet another cry for help. I secretly hoped they would tell someone, but of course they didn't. I felt more alone than I'd ever been.

Chapter Eight

After one particular rape, when I got smacked hard across the face because I had tried to refuse him, I knew I had to do something. It had come as a shock that he would abuse me that evening because Mum had only popped across the road to Eileen's house and had said she would only be five minutes. That was all he needed. I knew I would never be safe now.

That night I lay in bed and made plans. Well, I didn't actually make many plans: I simply decided to go, to run away. I didn't take anything with me. I climbed out of my bedroom window, across the kitchen roof and dropped into the back yard. Once I was out in the street, I had no idea where to go, so I walked about our area, looking in shop windows, shivering in doorways, until at about 4 a.m. a police patrol car drew up next to me.

I told them I was going to a friend's house, but when they asked where she lived, I said, 'I forgot.' They got the address in Knapp Road out of me, took me there, knocked on the door and woke Mum and Mick. Strangely, I didn't get beaten that night, but I got a big telling-off from Mum.

I was mentally very fragile at this time. I was convinced that there was someone standing in the corner of my bedroom, that a pool of shadow was a person. I was not frightened: I thought it was Jesus. I had been praying to him for years, and I believed he had given me different signs that, even in my worst suffering, he was there for me. I no longer went to church, but

I had a strong faith, probably born of the necessity of having something to keep me going through my dark times.

I was still trying to keep awake at night: I have never, ever had good sleep patterns, because I have always been frightened of surrendering to sleep. I was never sure when he would come. In Knapp Road he could sneak from the bedroom he shared with Mum into mine at any time, but he usually came after I'd gone to bed but while she was still downstairs. I became an expert on every creak of the floorboards, recognising them each by their different sounds. I would lie in bed, monitoring the house. If I heard someone come upstairs, I couldn't relax until I heard them go to the toilet and go back down again.

I began inventing alter egos for myself. If I met someone at Chrisp Street Market, which was close to our school and one of the markets where we regularly shopped, I'd give myself a different name and a different life: 'My dad spoils me rotten. Mum doesn't have to work because Dad looks after us all.' It was an idealised, happy life, and I did it because I found people reacted differently to me if I seemed to be happy. I had been told often enough that I looked miserable, so now I deliberately set out to dispel that image, even at the cost of the truth. I knew from experience it was no good telling people that I got battered at home: the world didn't want to know. I'd tried telling Mum's friend Eileen, Madeleine, a teacher at school, friends I made in the park. Some of them were sympathetic, but mostly their attitude was 'Don't tell me, I can't cope with it.' It was the early 1970s and domestic violence was still a big taboo.

I didn't tell Madeleine about the sexual abuse, but she knew how frightened I was of Mick Garvey. I can remember sitting in the cemetery with her once after school, and we were planning to write some poems together.

'Why don't we go to yours?' she asked.

'Mick the Prick is in,' I said.

She knew I hated him, and we both used that name for him.

'So?' she said.

'I can never take mates home. He beats me mother, and he'll make me look stupid in front of you. He's dead embarrassing.'

'If he says anything, I'll tell him what I think of him,' she replied firmly.

I gave a small, hopeless laugh. 'It's no good. We can't go there. Let's go to yours.'

How could I begin to explain to someone from a normal, happy family background what life was like at our house? Besides, it had been instilled in me from an early age, by my mum as well as Mick Garvey, that I should never tell others what happened. 'Don't you bloody well tell anyone,' Mum would say after he beat her up. 'I don't want no one feeling sorry for me.'

After my first failed attempt at running away, there were many more, during the day and at night. I never ventured further than the streets around our area, and the police got used to picking me up and taking me home. They didn't even have to ask for my address.

Mick's reaction was 'She's shagging about, that's why she's running off.' Then he'd give me a good hiding 'for bringing shame on the family'. He'd accuse me of 'bringing the police to our door', conveniently forgetting all the times they turned up to question him. He was still involved in minor criminal activities, and detectives were a familiar sight on the doorstep. We were given four chickens, which lived in our back yard. A local vicar had owned them but was moving and couldn't keep them. Mum heard about them, took them in and built a chicken run. Me and Tom had to feed them and clean them out. A big white one called Henry was so bold he used to walk into the kitchen and eat his corn in front of the fire.

It was underneath the chicken run that Mick used to stash anything he didn't want the police to find. There was a loose board in the floor, with straw on top of it. I can remember a couple of times when the police turned the place over and I was dying to point them in the right direction, but I never dared. They searched everywhere, but never looked under the hens.

Mick appeared to be convinced that I had become sexually active with lads outside the home. He was always accusing me of it publicly ('She's shagging about') and in private. When he was raping me, he would say, 'What do you get up to with that lad? Does he do this, or that? Does he make you feel as good as I make you feel?'

I kept denying it: I refused to feed his perverted fantasies. It certainly wasn't true. When I was out, I would hang around with a gang of lads, and get into minor bits of trouble, such as stealing sweets from shops, but I never got involved with drugs or alcohol, and I certainly wasn't sexually active. The thought of sex with anyone completely repelled me, and I had no boyfriends after Frankie.

My mum became worried about me running away and getting into trouble and eventually I was referred to social services. I think Mum rang them up and asked for help, but I can't remember exactly when it happened – I guess I was about thirteen or fourteen. Mick Garvey was furious that she had involved someone else in our problems. I was given a social worker, a young man, and I had to see him every week at Tower Hamlets Social Services office at Mile End, only a fifteen-minute walk from home. On the days I had to go, Mick would grab hold of me by the throat when nobody was around and say, 'Keep your fucking mouth shut when you go up there or they'll put you straight into care.'

Fearful of Mick's threat about going into care, the social worker would ask me if everything was all right and I would always say yes. I loved my mum and my brothers; I loved my school and my friend Madeleine; for them I would put up with Mick Garvey. I was also very worried about what would happen at home if I was not there: would he abuse one of my brothers? Would he murder Mum? I needed to be at home.

Soon after I started seeing the social worker, I began to feel very odd. My tummy was bloated, my breasts were tender, and I felt sick all the time. I missed my period and became worried. I knew something was wrong, but at the same time I naïvely thought I was too young to have a baby. It was only when I missed my period for a second month that I began to believe the worst had happened. Even then I kept thinking it would be all right, every morning hoping that I would find blood in my knickers. Eventually I told myself that if I didn't have a period by a certain date, I was definitely expecting a baby. And it would be my stepdad's. I felt completely trapped, with nobody to turn to. I couldn't tell my social worker or anyone else. I never thought about the baby inside me as a living creature, and I didn't feel any attachment to it. I was too bewildered, completely unsure of what to do and who to tell.

I was in bed one night, lying awake, certain that Mick would come because I had seen the telltale look in his eye earlier in the evening. When nobody was looking, he would wiggle his tongue at me lasciviously, which made me feel sick with apprehension. After Mum had been in bed some time, I heard the familiar creak of the uncarpeted floorboards on the landing, and he came in and raped me. He was never gentle with me, and that night he was rougher than usual, forcing himself deep inside me, clamping his hand across my mouth when I gasped with pain.

When he had finished, I felt a low pain in my stomach, like

a period pain but stronger. At first it kept me awake, but then an hour or two later, just as I had finally been drifting off, I had a terrible, much stronger pain in my stomach. I went to the toilet, thinking I needed to poo, but instead some black clumps of blood fell into the toilet bowl.

I didn't understand what was happening. I thought he had hurt me so badly that a piece of my insides had come away. I wanted to pick up the lumps and take them to a hospital and ask them to tell me which bits of me had been torn out, how badly he had damaged me, but I couldn't put my hand into the toilet. Usually when he raped me, I didn't bleed, so why was it happening this time? I crawled back to bed and put on a sanitary towel.

The next morning I was feverish and faint, so Mum kept me home from school. Luckily, Mick wasn't at home, and when Mum went to work, I put my bloodstained sheets in the washing machine. She knew I was ill, but she thought I was just having a heavy period and that my temperature was caused by a bug I'd picked up. I spent the day dozing, feeling tired and weak, taking paracetamol to ease the stomach cramps, and weeping.

The following day I felt a bit better and, as I knew Mick wasn't working, I insisted on going to school. The bleeding was dark and heavy for two or three days, and I was using wads of toilet roll as well as sanitary towels to soak it up, but to my relief it gradually became much lighter in colour and eventually stopped.

It was a couple of years later, when I heard of another girl losing a baby, that I fully understood that I had had a miscarriage. Until that moment I don't think I had allowed myself to confront the fact that I had been made pregnant by Mick. Looking back, I can see that by raping me that night he, perversely, did me a favour. What would I have done if the pregnancy had progressed? What kind of life would that poor child have had? I wouldn't have been able to accept a child that was half his, and I would have been taken into care. I was fighting so hard to hold on to my sanity at this stage in my life that a pregnancy would surely have tipped me over the edge.

A few weeks later I had another medical emergency. My tonsils, which had always given me trouble, literally exploded in my mouth one day while I was sitting in class at school. I was rushed to East Ham Memorial Hospital and operated on straight away. When I came round, Mum and Mick were both by my bedside, looking so concerned that at first I was convinced I must be dying. Mum was worried because I had just come out of major surgery, but he was scared that, in the hospital setting, something would emerge about the abuse. He had no chance to be on his own with me to reinforce his threats of what would happen if I told anyone. Three times over the next few hours he told Mum to go and get some tea, but each time she said, 'You get it. I'm not leaving her.' He was fuming. He couldn't issue his usual brutal commands to Mum, but nor could he find any means of getting her out of the way. He didn't need to worry: I was too well drilled in my fear of him to say anything to anyone.

Two weeks in hospital were for me like a holiday. The pain of having my tonsils out was a small price to pay for the sanctuary of the hospital. I was fed jelly and ice cream because my throat was so sore, and when I was able to walk about, I helped the nurses with the other patients. I was on an adult ward and most of the patients were elderly. I'd plump up pillows, help them eat and, as soon as my voice was strong enough, read to them. Best of all, I could climb into my bed at night and sleep safely. There were no doors, no creaking floor-boards, and there was always a dim light on above the nurses' station. If I woke during the night, the lovely nurses would make me tea and toast. I would think, Why can't home be more like hospital, cosy and warm and safe?

I had to stay off school for a week after I got home, which worried me. Luckily, Mick was working, but I'd spend all day praying, Please let Mum come home first. And she always did. But I knew that all emotions of relief and peace were short term – I could never really relax. I had to be prepared.

The days when he didn't touch me were almost as bad as when he did, because I'd have to stay awake all night. At least if he raped me, I could sleep a bit afterwards. At school, when other kids were running about or chatting their way through playtime and dinnertime, I'd find a quiet corner and sleep.

I was still running away, sometimes managing to evade the police for a couple of nights at a time. I was getting cleverer at not being found. I slept in hidden places. There weren't homeless people on the streets of London in any great numbers in those days, and certainly not around my area. One of my favourite places was Mile End Cemetery. It took me a while to pluck up the courage to sleep there, but then I told myself that dead people were the safest to be with as they couldn't harm me. Besides, I had always believed that my nan and Jesus were watching me, and a cemetery, with all its stone angels and carved pages from the Bible, felt a bit like a church. I found one tomb with a hole underneath the stone slab that I could slide into, leaving just my head and shoulders above the ground. I knew there were creepy-crawlies down there, but they didn't bother me.

I also found that I could sleep in phone boxes. I would lodge myself on the shelf and lift my feet up. Even though it wasn't comfortable, it was easier to sleep sitting down than standing up. And if I spent a night in a locked park, I always slept under the bench, never on top – it was more sheltered, and when the police had a quick glance around in the night, they didn't look underneath.

During the day I ate in supermarkets. I wandered around the aisles eating a pork pie or a sausage roll; I much preferred filling, savoury food to sweets and biscuits. Sometimes I went into a supermarket café, where I could take a drink from the dispenser without having to pass the till. I'd sit at a table drinking, and if I saw anyone leave without finishing their food, I'd move tables and eat their leftovers. I'd also wash and have a drink of water in supermarket toilets. When you are on the streets, clean drinking water is a precious commodity.

I only once got stopped, when one of the supermarket staff saw me pick up a banana and eat it. She said curtly, 'I hope you are going to pay for that.'

'Of course I am. I'll take the skin to the checkout.'

I had a pork pie in my pocket, but I put that back in case she was watching me. Then I dumped the banana skin behind some soap-powder boxes and left, moving on to another supermarket and another pork pie. There was a good selection of shops around where we lived, and I fed myself in all of them, as well as on the market when the traders' backs were turned.

If I saw anyone I knew during the day, I'd dodge away through the market or round a corner. I only talked to complete strangers, and to them I told different stories. It was at this time that I gave myself a new name: Sherry. I had no idea why I chose it; it came in a moment of inspiration. But looking back, I think I was trying to link back to the happiest time of my life, before Mick Garvey appeared, when I would go with Nan to the off-licence to buy her sherry, then cuddle up with her and watch television.

Inevitably the police would find me, I'd be taken home, and the social worker would be called. I can remember one occasion when the social worker was at the house, along with the police, and Mick Garvey was saying to him, 'Well, there's no problems with her home life. If there was, she'd have told you, wouldn't she? She's just being very wilful.' His audacity amazed me, but it only confirmed my belief that it was pointless telling anyone.

Once, I got caught sleeping under the bed of a lad I went to school with. He was just a mate and I'd been hanging around with the gang he was in. They all knew I had problems with my dad hitting my mother; her black eyes and bruises were no secret in the streets around Knapp Road. This lad sneaked me back into his house and brought me food, and I slept on the floor. But on the third day his mother heard a noise upstairs when he was out and came up to his room to catch a glimpse of my bottom wriggling under the bed. I thought I'd got away with it, but half an hour later the bedroom door burst open and his mum, my mum and Mick Garvey were there.

I heard his big, booming voice: 'Sharon, get out from under that bed.'

Here we go again, I thought resignedly. I'm going to get battered.

But I didn't. Mum was really upset, and the social worker turned up once more. The next morning Mum's friend Eileen, who had a phone, came over to tell Mum that social services were going to ring her in ten minutes. Mum insisted I go across to Eileen's house with her.

The upshot was that I was taken into temporary foster care over Christmas 1973. I was placed for a few weeks with a vicar and his family, to give my family a break. It really freaked Mick out. He tried to pretend he cared about me, saying to Mum, 'It's not right her being away from her family for Christmas,' but really he was terrified I would say something. Before I went, he grabbed me by my arm and pulled my face close to his and said, 'You keep your fucking mouth shut or you won't be coming back.'

I enjoyed my stay at the vicarage. The vicar and his wife were kind, and they had two small children whom I liked playing with. It was a lovely, peaceful Christmas, and I enjoyed all the trips to church. They gave me presents on Christmas Day, sensible things: gloves, a scarf and a woolly hat, knickers, a writing set. I didn't get anything from home, or have any contact with them. I didn't really miss them, but on Christmas Day I had a little pine for Tom and Phil. I was worried about Mum, too, knowing that over Christmas Mick would be drinking, which always made him more violent.

I was there for four weeks, and then it was back home, and back to my weekly visits to the social worker.

I was approaching my fourteenth birthday when I went on my regular visit to the social worker, and we had our usual conversation.

'How have you been?'

'Fine.'

'Have you had much sleep?'

It must have been clear that I hadn't. I was curled up in a foetal position in the chair, falling asleep.

'Sharon, I'm talking to you.'

'I know, I can hear you.'

'If you had a choice of anything in the world at this minute, what would it be?'

'To go to sleep and never wake up,' I answered bleakly.

I was fighting an overwhelming depression. Death was becoming a very seductive option and I thought about it all the time. It seemed the only way to end the pain. All that stopped me was fear for Mum and my brothers. I had worked out various ways of doing it, only to reject them. Hanging was out, because of the risk that Tom or Phil would find me. Slitting my wrists was too messy and painful. I'd heard someone talking about it, and I didn't think I could go through with it. The only possible way, I decided, was with tablets, so I hoarded paracetamol. I'd take a strip from every box that Mum bought and hide them inside my pillowcase. In my head, I wrote many suicide notes, but I never committed them to paper. I really believed I was going to have to kill myself, because I felt too bone-weary to carry on. With all my heart and soul I wanted to go to sleep and never wake up.

The social worker seemed surprised by my answer, and a little shocked. I think he had been expecting me to choose the latest stereo system, or clothes, or something like that. 'Why do you feel like that?' he asked.

It was the question I had been waiting for someone to ask me all my life. For once I took the bait. I think I was just too low to even think about the consequences. 'Because my dad keeps having sex with me and I can't do it no more.'

The words came out in a flat monotone. I was almost beyond feeling pain, or relief that I had spoken, or terror of Mick Garvey finding out that I had betrayed him. I simply wanted to die, and before I died I wanted to say what had happened. I felt beaten down, at rock bottom. I just wished someone would wrap me up and take me away from my whole life.

The look of surprise on the social worker's face turned to one of shock and disgust. His voice took on a very grave tone as he said, 'Do you know what will happen to you if you go around telling lies like that about your dad? You'll get him into serious trouble. Don't let me hear you talking like that again.'

He was the very first adult I had confided in, and his reaction confirmed everything that Mick Garvey had told me since I was four years old, everything that had been reinforced by the visit to the police station and the endless times Mum had believed him over me. I felt utter desolation. I stared blankly into the distance, not bothering to respond.

What's the point? I asked myself. I may as well be dead. Everything Mick Garvey says about nobody believing me is right. This social worker is meant to protect me, but he's not on my side at all.

To give the social worker the most benefit that I can possibly muster, he was probably only about twenty-eight and inexperienced. This was 1974, twelve years before the establishment of Childline and the public acceptance that sexual abuse happened in families.

At that moment, I just felt completely trapped.

Why am I fighting? Why don't I just give in? I asked myself, hopelessness washing over me.

So I did, and for the next twelve months I slumped into a deep lethargy. I became, for the only time in my life, a victim.

CHAPTER NINE

I stopped trying to fight. I stopped trying to save myself within my head. I stopped lying awake at night. I allowed it to happen, whenever and wherever he wanted. I really felt it was my fate and I had to surrender to it. I hated it, and I lay there rigid when he abused me, but I didn't try to avoid it or resist him. I simply told myself that the physical pain would soon be over.

I wouldn't go out. I was still friends with Madeleine at school, but I wouldn't meet her afterwards. I withdrew into the abuse, into life at home. I didn't want to mix with other people; I felt the dirt that was on me would rub off on to them. I cried a lot. Sad programmes on television made me cry, as did articles in newspapers. I cried for my nan. I cried for the sake of crying.

I hated myself.

I couldn't silence the negative thoughts in my head: Mum didn't want me when she got pregnant with me. She wanted a boy. My real dad said he would always love us, but where is he? Nobody can see what's happening, and if I tell them, they don't believe me.

It felt as though I had fallen into a black hole and nobody could see me falling. My self-esteem, never very high, was at rock bottom during these months.

Mum was glad that I was staying in more and concentrating on my schoolwork, but she would say, 'You're a miserable cow. You've never got a smile on your face, walking around like the worries of the world are on your shoulders. For God's sake, go out and have fun, have a laugh.'

Mick Garvey said, 'Leave her alone. At least she's not running away. She's in the house and we know where she is.' It suited him to have me around.

Sometimes I would dream about my real dad, but the memories of him were very faint, and there were times when I couldn't recall his face. I knew his name was Costain (I'd been called Garvey from the moment Mick had moved in), and I could remember that he worked in the docks, but I wasn't sure exactly what he did. Whenever I saw hoardings for Costain, the huge building company, I would fantasise that that was my dad, and that he had become rich and would come and save me in a big car, like a prince in a fairy tale.

In the subjects I enjoyed at school, I was working hard and doing well. I was still writing poetry, and my English teacher was so impressed that she suggested I get together with another girl, who wrote good stories, and publish a collection to raise money for school funds. I can remember the book; it had a blue cover and, though only stapled together, looked impressive. I designed the cover, which had the words 'Love, Hate, Rich, Poor, Home, Away' around the edge, and they were joined with lines to the middle. Our little book sold very well, and my teacher told Madeleine, 'One day Sharon will write a real book. She's got it in her.'

Paradoxically, it was a savage beating that Mick Garvey gave Mum that brought me out of my depression. She had to go to work wearing sunglasses to hide her black eyes, and it was raining. I felt such shame for her, and such pity. Please, God, don't let me live like that, I prayed. Then all my anger towards him flooded back, and my apathy was displaced. I'd been so tired, fighting him for years, and when the social worker hadn't believed me, it was as if my spirit had finally been broken, but now a surge of fury restored my strength.

I swear to You, God, that one day I will get him. I will remember every detail of what he has done to me, and one day I will make him pay.

I couldn't bear to watch my mother suffering, so I started to run away again. I was older, and better at it, and I managed to stay away longer. I liked being the fantasy me, Sherry, who existed when I was no longer under the same roof as Mick. I was a real storyteller, spinning a line to anyone I met. For me, the boundaries between lies and truth had become blurred years before, when the police sergeant had preferred to take Mick Garvey's word over mine. This had been compounded whenever Mum had supported him, and when the social worker had proved conclusively to me that my truths were everyone else's lies. I had learned that if you pretend hard enough that a lie is the truth, you can convince yourself enough to believe it.

Whenever I smell the damp woodsmoke aromas of autumn, it brings back to me my times as a runaway, when I wandered cold streets, feeling isolated and unloved, but at the same time enjoying the feeling of control; I could have chosen to stay home, warm and well fed but afraid, and instead I had chosen to be cold, hungry, alone and yet without fear. As I passed houses, I could see television sets flickering, and sometimes I glimpsed families eating their evening meal around a table. When it got late, I would climb into locked-up parks and settle on a bench or, if it was raining, lurk in a subway. I had learned that I made myself conspicuous, and more likely to be picked up by the police, if I carried on walking.

Once, after I'd been away a couple of days, the police found me and held me in a cell. They told me they had phoned for my social worker to come, the man who I had once entrusted with my huge secret and who had let me down so bitterly. I went into hysterics and said I wouldn't allow him near me, so after that I was assigned a different one, a woman. She still took me back home, so nothing had changed. Mick gave me a good hiding when I was brought back, and then abused me the next night.

He was very confident by now. He'd seen me in the hands of the police, social workers, teachers and in hospital, and as far as he knew I'd never told anyone. There had been no repercussions. He became more blatant about his abuse, though he was still careful to keep it away from Mum, Tom and Phil. Mum knew I hated him, and when he was out, she would say, 'Sharon, when he gets in, don't antagonise him, don't cause arguments. He'll only drag you upstairs and give you a good hiding.'

If he had only been giving me a good hiding, I would have put up with it, for her sake. I wanted to make the world better for her, and I felt very guilty because I really believed I was to blame for all our family's problems.

Madeleine and the other girls at school were into clothes and make-up, and they had great fun experimenting with their looks. For me, anything to do with making myself look more grown-up or more attractive was very frightening. It was sexualising me, and I didn't want to be a sexual person. I covered the walls of my bedroom with pictures of the squeaky-clean Donny Osmond and the androgynous Marc Bolan, and concentrated my longings on them. They were remote, unreal, never going to be part of my life, so it was safe for me to like them and feel attracted to them. I was still scruffy and smelly, and boys at school only befriended me as a means of getting to my best friend, Madeleine, who everyone fancied.

Although my attendance record at school was not good – I

missed loads when I was running away – and I only worked for the teachers and on subjects that I liked, I was still doing remarkably well, and as my sixteenth birthday loomed, in March 1976, so did my GCEs, a couple of months later.

My English teacher, Mrs White, took me to one side and said she was really keen that I carry on with my education after the GCEs, taking A levels and getting into teacher training college. She told me I would make a great English teacher, as I had the language and the imagination, and I was able to draw people into my stories and poems. She even said they would be thrilled if one day I came back to teach at the school. I told her I would love to. In my head I had visions of college, living in a dormitory, away from home, with new friends and a new life. I skipped home happily to pour out the news to Mum, who was almost as excited as I was.

Mum broke the news to Mick over dinner that the school felt I had good prospects.

'She can fuck off if she thinks I'm going to provide for her while she swans around college all day,' he sneered. 'I'm not working my bollocks off to keep her – the answer is no.'

Mum argued and argued – she really did try to stand up to him – but it made no difference. Just like that Mick crushed my dreams. You never could persuade Mick Garvey to change his mind. I told my teacher that, regretfully, I wouldn't be able to carry on with my education.

The school was not giving up on me, though. My head of year, Mr Cockett, came round to our house one day after school to try to persuade my parents. He was a science teacher, gangly, with glasses and a great sense of humour. When I walked into school late, he'd say things like, 'Oh, Garvey's late again. Don't tell me – a dinosaur fell out of the sky and stood in your way and wouldn't let you come to school.' He'd say it good-naturedly and it'd always make me smile.

I'd quip back, 'Sir, you were there! Why didn't you save me?'

When Mum opened the door to him, he explained who he was and said he wanted to talk to them about my future. Mick came to the door and gave him short shrift: he never even got across the doorstep.

When Mrs White heard, she determined to have another go and made an appointment to see Mum and Mick the following Friday after school. She said she would explain to them how, with grants, it would cost very little for them to let me go to college.

When Friday came, I rushed home, feeling excited and sick at the same time. Fifteen minutes later my teacher was shown into the living room. I crept part way downstairs to listen and could see Mrs White through the half-open door. She said, 'Sharon has the brains to do this, she has the ability, and it would be such a great shame if she missed this opportunity. She could have a very good career, Mr and Mrs Garvey. Surely you want the best for her?'

But he was having none of it: 'She's my daughter and I've kept her all these years and I don't intend to keep her any longer. She's old enough to get out and work. The answer is no. It's always going to be no. You're wasting your time.'

Mum tried to speak: 'If her school thinks she could do it, Mick—'

He banged his fist down on the table so hard that Mrs White jumped up in fright. He continued angrily, 'I've made my decision. She's not going to college. Now get out of my house.'

Mrs White nodded and gathered her things. As she was leaving, she said, 'It is your decision, Mr Garvey, but Sharon starts her GCEs next month and we are expecting her to pass with good grades in some of her subjects.'

'She won't be passing nothing 'cos she isn't sitting no exams or going back to school. So good day to you.' He slammed the door shut, then bellowed for me to come downstairs.

I crept downstairs, feeling hopeless.

'What are you doing sending that bitch round here?' he roared. 'You've already had one teacher here – wasn't that enough? You bring nothing but trouble to this door. I don't know why I've kept you as long as I have. I should have had you put away years ago.'

I knew now that my dream was over. I could never escape him. If I didn't get a good education, how would I ever have enough money to leave home? And I loved school: it was my refuge, the place I felt safe and happy. I wanted to be educated, I wanted a decent life, I wanted to live in a different way. Now all hope of that had gone. A feeling of deep misery descended on me. My escape hatch had been closed. He had done what he always did: destroyed every chance of happiness.

Later that night Mum had to go to work. Tom had taken Phil out with him, and I sat in my bedroom dreading what was to come. The door flew open.

'Thought you were clever, bitch, did you?' he sneered venomously. He grabbed my hair, yanked me off the chair and onto the bed. 'You try anything like that again and I will make your life a thousand times worse than it is now. Do you understand?'

I nodded mutely as he began unbuckling his belt.

Is he going to beat me, or is he going to rape me?

I soon found out. He pushed me flat on the bed, winding his hand into my hair to force me back and hold me in place, and pulling my pyjamas and knickers off with the other hand. I didn't struggle: the fight had completely gone out of me. He raped me, his way of letting me know that he was in control of my life and that nothing would ever free me. All my efforts to change things, to give myself a future, were cast aside by this brute of a man who was astride me, treating me as his own personal plaything.

He was raping me up to six times a week at this stage of my life. He was also molesting me at other times. Even if other people were in the house, if he was on his own in a room with me, he'd push me up against a wall and grope my breasts. If there was nobody around, he'd force me to perform oral sex.

He and Mum were fighting all the time, mostly about his womanising. He'd go out for a drink and come back at 2.30 a.m. reeking of perfume. Perversely, I was happy that he was seeing other women. Not because I wanted Mum to be unhappy, but I just always hoped he'd find another woman stupid enough to let him move in with her and that he'd leave us.

Perhaps to try to make it up to me for my disappointment about school, when my sixteenth birthday came round Mum asked if I wanted a party. I said yes, but deep inside I never thought it would happen. Again Mick objected, but this time she got her way. She wanted to celebrate the fact that I was grown-up, so she dug her heels in. All my classmates were invited, and some other friends of Madeleine's. It was only when the day itself dawned that I really believed it would happen, and that's when my tummy filled with butterflies of excitement. Nothing so wonderful had ever happened to me before. I'd never had a party, not even as a little girl.

Mum laid on a wonderful spread of food and spent hours helping me get ready. She bought me new clothes, insisted I had a bath, washed and curled my hair, and did my make-up. When I looked in the mirror, I couldn't believe it was me: I'd never imagined that I could be pretty. I looked stunning, so different from the scruffy, smelly Sharon everyone knew.

With the thrill of all the preparations, I forgot my problems and couldn't wait for 7 p.m. to come. Mum and Mick went out to the pub, and the arrangement was that they would return at

11 p.m., when the party would end. Phil went to sleep at a neighbour's, and Tom stayed at the party.

I can still remember vividly those awkward few minutes before anyone turned up, that sickening feeling that perhaps nobody would come. But by ten past seven they were all arriving, dressed up for the party. The biggest thrill came as they each did a double take when they saw me: my transformation was amazing, and came as a real surprise to everyone.

We had music on in the living room for dancing, and food and drink – only pop, of course – in the kitchen. (The kitchen was no longer dangerous, as Mum had a few months earlier, after three years living as squatters, forced the council to recognise us as tenants, and we were now paying rent and had a safe electricity supply.)

It was all so innocent, and I was very happy. Some of the kids at the party were the ones who had bullied me. Now they could see me in a different light. Everyone was having a great time, dancing, flirting, kissing. Nobody was behaving wildly or badly, and it was all very innocent. I sat on the stairs, about halfway up, with a boy from school. He told me how pretty I was, and he leaned over and kissed me gently on the lips. He was one of the cool, good-looking lads, and he'd never given me a second glance before. I was beginning to relax and really enjoy myself, thrilled with the attention, and proud to be hosting such a good party. The problems of my home life receded, and for the first time in my life I was one of the gang, a normal teenager.

Suddenly the front door banged open, crashing back on its hinges with a judder, and the huge bulk of Mick Garvey loomed in the hallway. 'What the fucking hell are you doing upstairs, you little slag?' he yelled at me, his coarse voice booming through the house. 'Get down here.' He turned to Mum, who had followed him in, looking worried and sheepish.

'Look, Sandra, she's been shagging about with boys upstairs. I told you she would. This is why we had to come home.' Then he turned on me again. 'Get down here, you slut. You're a filthy bitch. Your mother stupidly said we could trust you, but I knew better, you dirty little cow.' His face was red and contorted with rage.

I could see the shock on my friends' faces. The music was switched off, and everyone began to sidle self-consciously towards the door, grabbing their coats as they went. I froze to the spot, humiliated and desolate. As quickly as they could, everyone left, some of them shooting me looks of pity and whispering goodbye to me. I stared at the floor, unable to face them. It was only 9 p.m., but according to what Mum told me later, he'd been itching to come back from the moment they had reached the pub.

I'll never dress up and make myself look nice again, I told myself miserably. I knew that if I did, something terrible would happen.

Mum quickly hustled me up to my room, trying to keep the peace. 'Get up to bed now. I'll calm him,' she said.

I lay on my bed in abject misery for a few minutes, then ripped off my new dress and threw it across the room. In the bathroom I scrubbed and scrubbed to get the make-up off my face, making my skin red raw. I doused my hair with water to make it straight again. Being pretty Sharon doesn't work. Nothing in my life works, I told myself over and over.

Back in my room, I thought longingly of death, peace, being out of it all. Inevitably, some time in the early hours, when the rest of the house was sleeping, he came to my room.

'Filthy little whore. Thought you could slag around with boys, did you?' he snarled before raping me.

How can I describe the rape? There were so many it was routine for me, and as ever I shut my mind away from what was happening to my body. Thank God I was able to live elsewhere in my head.

The next day nothing was said about my party. It was always like that in our house. There would be terrible fights and rows, Mum would get battered, and once morning came, it was all forgotten.

I had to brace myself to face my classmates at school the following Monday. I felt so ashamed, and shame made me feel isolated. But to my surprise, I got a lot of sympathy. Until then, nobody apart from Madeleine had a clue how terrible my home life was, and now at least they knew a small part of the horror story. They were all very nice to me, and nobody said anything nasty. Even the bullies treated me differently.

Very soon after the fiasco of my sixteenth birthday Mick announced that he had found me a job working at Liptons' teashop in Whitechapel. He told me on a Friday and I had to start on the Monday. And so, three months before I was legally supposed to and before I could take my GCEs, I left school. I didn't even have the chance to say goodbye.

The shop sold specialist teas and coffees, and there was a cold meat counter. I earned £12.60 a week, and I had to hand over my wage packet to him unopened. He handed back £2, which covered my bus or tube fare for the week. Mum made me a sandwich to take with me. He pocketed the rest of my money, saying that it was his because he had got me the job.

I hated it. I hated being bossed around, the other staff treated me like dirt, I hated serving customers, and I didn't even get a share of the money I was earning. After four or five weeks I stopped going. I didn't dare tell anyone at home, so I went out every day with my sandwich as usual. I'd walk the streets, sit in the library reading books or meet up with my friends who were still at school. Oh, I was so envious of them!

They moaned and groaned about revision for GCEs, but I'd have done it so willingly.

When payday came round, I was terrified but concocted a story about losing my pay packet on the way home. Mick was angry, and there were three days of arguments in the house because he believed I'd pocketed the money, and he still had to give me the £2 for my fares. All week I dreaded the next payday, and eventually, in terror, I owned up to Mum. She told him and he went ballistic. Now that I was bigger, he didn't hit me as much as he had done, and if he did, I could resist him better. It wasn't so much that I fought back, but I had learned how to protect myself. He swore at me and announced that he would get me another job.

That night, while raping me, he spat in my ear with menace, 'You might never have to work again.'

He didn't normally talk to me, apart from calling me filthy names and threatening me if it seemed like I might make a noise.

'What?' I asked, not understanding what he meant.

'I'll get you a little flat. I could bring people to visit you. You'd make a few bob that way,' he whispered.

'What?' I was still baffled, unwilling to take in what he had said.

'What I do to you – you could get twenty quid a time for doing it with other blokes. We'd go fifty-fifty.'

He spoke as though it was normal, just like he was talking about another job for me. It took a few seconds to sink in, but when I realised what he was proposing, I said defiantly, 'Never.'

'You'll fucking do what you're told,' he hissed.

That's prostitution, I thought, my mind racing. He's going to sell me. I've got to face reality now.

Nothing more was said that night, but I was terrified. I'd seen his friends, the kind of lowlifes who had hung around the

Harvey Hotel with him. I didn't want to associate with them in any way, let alone be forced to have sex with them. I knew I had to escape one way or another, and again I seriously considered suicide.

While I was working out what to do, Mum received a letter from the council offering us rehousing in a maisonette in Ackroyd Drive, just round the corner. The upheaval of the move distracted Mick from doing anything about me, and for a few weeks I wasn't working, just helping Mum. In retrospect it was such a shame: even if he hadn't allowed me to stay on at school to take A levels, I could at least have taken my GCEs.

It was a three-bedroom home, and there was one wonderful thing about it: the blind on the kitchen window didn't quite reach the bottom, so from outside you could look straight through the ground floor of the house. This meant I was safe downstairs, even if there was nobody else in the house. I again had my own room. I would lie in bed at night, making plans. I would switch between wanting to kill myself and dreaming of going somewhere nobody knew me, getting a job and a flat, and then bringing Tom and Phil to live with me. Eventually Mum would leave him and come to live with us.

Suicide seemed the only real option, the only one I could be sure would work. I finally decided to do it after a double rape: he raped me in bed at night, while mum was working at the pub, and again the next morning, after the boys had gone to school and Mum had again gone to work. It was particularly cruel as after one rape I felt safe, usually for at least twenty-four hours, so to be caught again so soon was horrible. Being unemployed played into his hands: I was more available, and this was another reason I knew I had to get away.

That evening he and Mum went out, and I was babysitting Phil. I was afraid Mum would come home drunk, which always gave Mick an opportunity to rape me. I couldn't stand it any more, so I went around the house collecting all the tablets I could find. I still had my own stash of paracetamol, but I found more in the bathroom and in Mum's room. I took all the pills I could find, including her contraceptives, and put them in front of me on the kitchen table. I was crying, really sorry for myself and sorry to be leaving my brothers, but I was determined to do it then, because I wanted to be sure it was Mick and Mum who found me, not the boys.

I fetched a pint glass of water and made up my mind to swallow everything, then move to the settee to watch television until I died. Tears poured down my face as I pictured my own death scene, and I was glad that Mum would be pissed, so that it wouldn't hit her so hard.

I slumped on the sofa and started to swallow the tablets, my face wet with tears. Just then the front door burst open and Mum and Mick came in, in the middle of a blazing row. When she saw what I was doing, Mum completely lost control and started beating me, hitting me and screaming, 'Why are you doing this to me? There's something wrong with you. You're mad. You need a psychiatrist. Are you fucking thick?'

She was so beside herself that in the end Mick had to pull her off me. He had gone white, no doubt thinking that this was so serious that everything was going to come out. Her hurt and disappointment in me were crushing.

In the end she said, 'Get yourself up them stairs to bed and we'll talk in the morning.'

I was relieved. I thought at last I was going to have the opportunity to talk to her; she was going to sit me down and ask what was the root of my trouble. You ask me, I thought, just ask me. I'm ready to tell you now. But the next morning it wasn't mentioned, and life went on as if nothing had happened, just as it always did in my family. I found out later that Mum did tell my social worker, so she was trying to get help for me.

Mick didn't rape me the night I tried to commit suicide, but it didn't stop him for long. He must have felt invincible: once again, my desperate plea for help had been ignored. He could get away with anything. Some of the time I fought back; other times I did what I had done as a small child and just willed it to be over as quickly as possible, retreating into my head.

With his lorry-driving job he was often around for days at a time, and because I wasn't working there were more opportunities, which he took gleefully. Every day I thought, You did it yesterday, so you won't do it today. But he did, and each time I felt more and more battered down by it, until in the end I felt I was going mad.

One night as he thrust himself on me, I struggled hard, shouting out, 'You're hurting me. Stop it!'

He clamped his hand over my mouth, but I tried to bite it and continued to make panicky sounds. Suddenly the rape was interrupted by a loud banging on the wall, and Tom's voice shouting, 'Leave her alone! Leave her alone!'

Tom saved me that night, because the minute Mick Garvey realised my brother was awake, he climbed off me and left the room. Tom never mentioned it the next day, and I thought he must have been half asleep when he did it.

I couldn't rely on Tom, who was only fourteen and a half, to be my saviour. I finally realised that I was never going to get help from outside: there was only one person who could stop him, and that was me.

Soon after that night he once again crept along the landing in the night and let himself into my room. This time I thought, No, you've done this for the last time. I don't care if you murder me. I don't care who knows what you're doing. If you kill me, Tom can protect Mum and you'll go to prison for ever and they'll be safe. You're doing me a favour – you're saving me from committing suicide.

'Your mum will be home in two hours. Tom's out. Move over,' he said.

'No. You're not doing anything to me any more.' I jumped up.

He was momentarily rocked. I, too, was shocked by my own defiance. It felt scary, but I was also determined to stick to it. One way or another it was going to end, even if I had to die.

'You fucking what?' he bellowed, trying to regain the upper hand.

'I'm telling Mum, the police, Uncle Gordon and I'll find my real dad one day and tell him.'

He grabbed me forcefully, pinioned me to the bed and started punching me with savage rage. The beating was merciless and I lost consciousness. When I came to, he was gone. I could barely see, but I knew there was blood all over the bed and the pillow. I stumbled towards the mirror and was shocked by what I could make out: one eye was so bruised, purple and yellow, that I couldn't see out of it at all; the other was partially closed, very bloodshot and also blackened. My lip was cut and swollen, and my nose was caked with dried blood, obviously caused by a nosebleed. When I tried to move, my whole body ached, and when I looked down, I could see more bruising on my arms and ribcage. My nightie was off, and I could tell from the familiar slimy feeling between my legs that I had been raped while unconscious.

Trying to stop myself shaking, I gingerly bathed my swollen face and washed away the blood. It made little difference: my face still looked terrible, distorted with swelling. Then, with shaking hands, I pulled out one of my treasured school exercise books and wrote a letter to Mum. I can remember almost exactly what I wrote:

> Dear Mum,
> I am so, so sorry I have caused you so much trouble, but I have been keeping secrets for many years, since I was a little girl. Your husband, Mick Garvey, has been raping me since I was very young and I can't take it any more. That's why I have tried to commit suicide, and why I have run away so much. I promise you I am now gone for good. I won't be back until he is gone for ever. I love you very much, and I tried my best to stay as long as I could.
> Love, Sharon

I don't know why but I dressed in my school uniform – perhaps it was because school to me symbolised happiness. I pulled the bedding over to cover the blood, confident that Mum would see it before anyone else. Then I tiptoed downstairs. He was in their bedroom, and I assumed he was asleep. I left the note where Mum would see it when she came in, then left. All I had with me were a carrier bag with my purse, a picture of Mum, Tom and Phil and a clutch of letters from Donna.

I walked to the nearest main road, Devons Road, and thumbed a lift from a man and woman, who took me to Brent Cross. I must have looked a shocking sight, but they didn't question me. Then I made my way to the bottom of the M1 and again tried to thumb a lift. Nobody stopped for me this time: I'm not surprised when I think back to how I looked. Eventually I wandered back to Brent Cross, caught a night bus to Aldgate East and walked back to Chrisp Street, to home territory.

I knew, from the many hours I had spent wandering the

area when I was playing truant or running away, that there was a Salvation Army property near the market, and on impulse I went there and rang the bell. After a long wait a little old lady unbolted it and opened up. She took one look at my bruised and swollen face and ushered me in. I felt safe just looking at her: she was homely, grey-haired, softly spoken.

She took me into an office and shortly afterwards a man in a Salvation Army uniform came in. He was Colonel Pratt, and he spent a long time talking to me, gently getting me to tell him all the details of my childhood and the abuse. I remember thinking, I've told Mum, so I might as well tell everyone. Surely someone will believe me.

He asked me about my real father, and I told him that, as far as I knew, he lived in Liverpool, but I had no idea where.

The old lady made a bed up for me in a side room. It was a narrow camp bed, but to me it was luxury because I knew I was safe. I slept for a long time, and when I woke the next day, she brought me delicious hot food. She was gentle and caring, and asked how I was feeling.

In the afternoon Colonel Pratt told me they had located my father in Liverpool and that he wanted to see me. I don't know how they found him so quickly, but the Salvation Army is famous for tracing people. A woman in army uniform took me to Euston Station, bought me a ticket and put me on a train for Liverpool. She gave me sandwiches and a flask, and told me how worried she was that I was travelling alone.

I was terrified at the prospect of meeting my dad after all these years. What if I don't recognise him? I asked myself. Will he be like Mick? Will he love me?

But mixed with the terror was a feeling of real elation. As the countryside whistled past the train window, I was putting many miles between myself and Mick Garvey, and I was heading back to the place I really considered home: Liverpool.

CHAPTER TEN

I felt excited and apprehensive as the train pulled into Lime Street Station. It was early evening, and still light. I needn't have feared I wouldn't recognise my dad. I knew him instantly, despite not having seen him for twelve years. He was older and had less hair, but otherwise he was exactly as he had been in my memory. He knew me too.

'God, girl, what's been happening to you?' he asked in shock as he looked at my battered face. He took me in his arms and gave me a hug.

I instantly felt comfortable with him. He had married again, and his wife, Margaret, was with him at the station. She hugged me too. 'You look as though you've been through the wars,' she said.

They took me home to the two-bedroom flat where they were living with Margaret's two sons, Stephen and Chris, and their baby daughter, Claire, who had been born with spina bifida and had many problems. I fell in love with her instantly. She was like a little doll.

That first evening when we walked in, Dad said frankly, 'What's all this about?'

He had already been told by the Salvation Army that I had been physically and sexually abused.

'He's been doing it for years, and I can't take it any more,' I said. Then I poured out my story. I didn't give details of what Mick Garvey had actually done to me, but told them enough for them to see how serious it was.

I cried, Dad cried, and Margaret sniffled as she made the tea. Dad believed me: he knew what a brute Mick Garvey was, but he was very shocked to hear about the sexual abuse.

'Don't worry now – you're safe with me.'

For me, just being believed by someone, an adult, was wonderful. In many ways, it was the most important thing. It was one small victory over my stepfather, who had always said nobody would believe me.

My dad didn't call the police, and I know he has always regretted that. I think he believed that as I was now safe, he was saving me from another ordeal – police interviews and court cases. But I was aware that the Salvation Army colonel hadn't called the police either, and in my mind this confirmed the invincibility of Mick Garvey. He was untouchable. Even though I was now believed, nothing would happen. Nobody seemed to share my fears that although I was out of his clutches, my brothers were still living there, and my mum was still being beaten up by him whenever he pleased.

Perhaps they think it is partly my fault, I wondered. Perhaps they think I should have done something earlier. Perhaps they think I enjoyed it.

I was tortured by these thoughts.

Dad and Margie had a lovely flat in Bootle, but space was tight. The two boys doubled up in the bottom bunk, and I slept on top. Being with them helped me over my homesickness because Chris was more or less the same age as Phil. I enjoyed helping to look after them and little Claire. Best of all, I saw Donna again. We had never lost touch, writing to each other throughout the years, and I'd phone her whenever I could. I had rung her from Euston Station to tell her I was coming back to Liverpool, and now we picked up together as if there had been five minutes, not five years since we'd last seen each other.

She cupped my poor, bruised face in her hands, and tears coursed down her cheeks as she told me how much she hated Mick Garvey and how she had always prayed for the day I would be finally free of him. I felt bad, remembering how she had cried for me when we were little and I had first told her about the abuse.

Why do I always bring such unhappiness to my best friend in all the world? I asked myself.

I made her swear she would tell nobody, not even her mother, where I was. I thought Mum and Mick would be looking for me, now that Mum knew the truth, and I had no wish to be found. I wouldn't find out for another ten years that after I had run away, Mick Garvey had destroyed the letter I had written for Mum and had changed the bloodstained sheets.

My stay with Dad and Margie was a wonderful respite, a time to gather my strength, let my bruises heal, learn to relax and sleep again. But it couldn't last: the flat was too cramped, and after a couple of months I heard them arguing about me. It wasn't the first time. Margie complained about having another mouth to feed and not enough money coming in. I felt I was putting a strain on them, and they had enough to cope with worrying about baby Claire.

Guilt was a familiar feeling for me: I had always felt guilty about the trouble I brought to Mum. Now I was feeling guilty about the trouble I was imposing on Dad and his family. I didn't want to spoil their lives. It was time, I felt, to stand on my own. I wrote them a letter thanking them for everything they had done, telling them not to worry about me and asking them to give Claire and the boys a hug from me. I crept out of the flat in the middle of the night.

I was frightened, and I knew that I was giving up a warm home, with food on the table and people who loved me, for a terrifyingly empty future, but I also knew how to live rough and that I could cope. As I walked away from the flat, there were tears in my eyes because I felt I may never see my dad again. Years later I found out that he had tried to find me, without success: I was becoming good at covering my tracks.

I made my way to the centre of the city, an area I knew well from our time living at the Harvey Hotel. I planned to find an alleyway where I could sleep, but I was cold and went first into a café for a cup of coffee. In there I met two women, who I could see straight away were twins. They were chatty and friendly, and when I said I had nowhere to stay, they offered to take me in. They told me they worked nights. I quickly realised, from my experience at the Harvey, that they were prostitutes.

They had a two-bedroom flat just off the docks road, and they happily moved together into one room and gave me the other. They told me they would feed and clothe me if, in return, I would clean the flat and do the washing. It seemed like a great deal to me, and I happily agreed. They spoiled me rotten. I can only remember one of their names, Marian, because she was the twin I preferred. They bought me clothes and did my hair for me. It was like living with two mums and no dad, and for me, that was the perfect situation.

They were very keen to warn me of the dangers of prostitution, but I was curious about what they did. I couldn't see the harm in it – they were funny, happy; they had good money and a lovely flat. It didn't seem to have done them any harm. I don't think I ever seriously considered doing it, but I wanted to know more about their lives, and one night I followed them down the docks road to a pub.

When they saw me walk in, they went mad. It was a rough place, full of seamen and hard-looking women. An innocent, fresh-faced sixteen-year-old wandering in caused a sensation:

the men were all looking at me, and the twins grabbed me and frogmarched me out before any of them could approach me.

Marian took me back to the flat and gave me a ticking-off. 'Don't you ever come down here again,' she warned. 'I mean it. Learn from me – don't wreck your life.'

A couple of weeks later the twins failed to come home. I didn't realise that they had been arrested, a fairly routine occurrence in the life of a docks prostitute. I felt abandoned, and unsure what to do. When they still hadn't returned the following evening, I formulated a naïve plan. The docks were just down the road, so I decided to stow myself away on a liner and go to America, where nobody would know me and I could start afresh.

I managed to slip into the docks unnoticed and up the gangplank of a huge liner that was berthed there. I was downstairs, below decks, wandering along what seemed like miles of corridors, when I came to some double doors. I opened them and found myself in a large stateroom. It was a living room with an adjoining bedroom and bathroom. In the bedroom was a long built-in wardrobe. I decided to hide in there. It was full of clothes, and on the floor beneath them were some boxes. I planned to stay there until we reached America: I had no idea of the length of the journey, thinking it was only a day or two.

Out of boredom I rummaged in some of the boxes, and in one found a large box of chocolates, which I opened and started to eat. In another box was some glittering jewellery: diamond bracelets, necklaces, rings, watches. I was particularly thrilled with some pretty jade earrings, which I clipped on my ears. I heard the ship's horn sound, and the engines begin to throb. Full of chocolates and lulled by the sound, I fell asleep.

The next thing I knew the wardrobe door was opened and

a hand came in and grabbed me by the scruff of my neck. Then another hand grabbed my arm, and I was pulled free. There were four men in front of me: the captain, another officer and two river police. I was gobsmacked to see the police uniforms. I thought we would be miles out to sea by now. I felt an overwhelming surge of disappointment. It looked as though another of my dreams was collapsing.

To this day I have no idea how they knew I was in the cupboard, but perhaps one of the passengers living in the stateroom had opened the door, seen me asleep and quietly closed it before summoning help.

'Do you know it's illegal to stow away?' one of the policemen asked me.

'Yeah.'

'So what are you doing here?' he questioned.

'I need to start a new life,' I said honestly.

'Well, we're taking you back to the docks. You're under arrest.'

I was frightened and had no idea what would happen to me. To get off the liner, I had to climb down a rope ladder on to a police launch. To my surprise, the policemen were gentle and kind. I think they felt sorry for me. They told me the liner was bound for Africa, which was a shock.

I said, 'All liners go to America, don't they?'

They shook their heads and explained what trouble a young girl on her own would have been in if she had managed to get all the way to Africa.

I was taken to the police station and spent the night there. It was not uncomfortable: my cell door was left open, and the policeman in charge brought me hot chocolate and a meal, and even played cards with me. Everyone was very kind. Someone went out and bought me a toothbrush and toothpaste, and I was able to have a good wash before I was taken to court the next day.

I travelled to Liverpool Magistrates Court in a van with separate cages inside, one for each prisoner. My fellow travellers were prostitutes and drunks, but I didn't talk to them. In court I was charged with theft of the chocolates and the earrings. Although it was my first time in a courtroom, I didn't feel frightened. The kindly policeman had told me they wouldn't send me to prison, so I thought that the worst that could happen to me would be to be taken into care, and at least that would mean I was fed and had a roof over my head.

Little did I know something much worse was in store for me. I was given a three-month suspended sentence and one of the conditions was that I had to return to London to live with my mother. The court social workers had traced her and made contact, and the magistrates were told she was willing to have me back. Nevertheless, I was convinced at this point that Mum would have read my letter and Mick Garvey would be history, so I didn't feel desolate. I was even quite excited at the prospect of seeing her, Tom and Phil again. But I did feel a strong sense of failure: nothing I tried to do to better myself ever worked. I took one step forward and two back.

A social worker put me on the train to London at Lime Street, a direct train that didn't stop, lest I jump off at the first opportunity. When we reached Euston, another social worker was on the platform, and although I had never seen him before, he recognised me, probably from a photograph.

'Hello, Sharon. Give us your bag,' he said. 'I'm taking you home to your mum and dad.'

As he said the words 'and dad', my stomach lurched. He's still there, I thought, a wave of nausea rising in my throat. It will all happen again. Maybe this is my fate, to be abused for ever. Please, God, just let him kill me, then it will all be over.

The social worker made small talk about the traffic and the weather. I said nothing. I'm sure he thought I was being sullen and difficult, but my mind was reeling. Dear Jesus, why have I got to suffer like this? Am I being taught a lesson? What did I do wrong?

As we turned into Ackroyd Drive, I felt physically sick. Any pleasure at the prospect of seeing Mum and my brothers was gone, and all I was aware of was a deep dread of seeing my stepfather.

The social worker came in and had a cup of tea with Mum, chatting amiably. My brothers were still at school.

All Mum said to me was, 'What have you been up to? Go and get a wash and I'll do you something to eat.'

I'd been away for three months, but she acted as though I had popped out an hour earlier. It was always the same: ignore a problem and it will go away.

At the top of the landing, I looked along to my own room. I felt no joy to be back. I was briefly tempted to tell her again what I had said in the letter, but I thought she must have chosen not to believe it, so what was the point? I had screwed up the courage, out of desperation after that last terrible beating, to write it all out for her, but I couldn't actually say the words 'Your husband has been having sex with me since I was a little girl.' She would hate me if I said it out loud: either because she thought I was lying or because I hadn't said or done anything earlier. There was nothing to do but accept my fate.

My brothers came in and were pleased to see me, but I think they also dreaded my presence, because of all the trouble that came with it. My stepfather walked in halfway through the evening.

'That bitch is here again, is she? You back then?' he sneered, turning to me. 'Been out selling yourself?'

I didn't argue or answer back, but hung my head as if I was ashamed. He had all the cards in his hand. At that moment I really felt there were two gods: the real God, who looked after me and was keeping me safe, and this man, who thought he was god but who destroyed everything around him.

That first night he didn't touch me, but on the second evening, when the boys were out with their friends and Mum was working, serving behind the bar of a pub in Leabridge Road, he walked into the living room while I was watching TV.

'You think you're fucking clever, don't you? The trouble you're causing in this house. But you'll never beat me, you know that, don't you?' he spat viciously.

He grabbed my head and made me give him oral sex. He literally forced my head up and down with his hands, making me feel he was going to break it right off my neck. I had my eyes closed tight and was saying over and over to myself, I can't live like this. This time I'm going for good.

The following night I sneaked out again, with a carrier bag full of clothes and a handbag containing my personal things. I hitched a lift from a man who dropped me at the nearest bus-stop where I could get a night bus. I managed to get to Brent Cross, then walked to the start of the M1, where I shivered in the cold rain as I tried to hitch a lift north. Nobody stopped for me, and after a while I was so tired I put the carrier bag on the ground and my handbag on top, and sat on them while I carried on thumbing. I must have looked a dejected little bundle.

After what seemed like an eternity, a big lorry pulled over and started to reverse up the hard shoulder towards me. I was delighted and jumped up and climbed up into the cab next to the driver. I was so grateful to get out of the rain and the cold that I completely forgot about my bags. We were miles up the motorway before I remembered them. The lorry driver said he was headed for Scotland, and that was fine by me: I wanted to go to Liverpool again, and he could get me well on my way.

What happened next I only heard about much later. It seems that the wind carried my bags on to the motorway, and the contents of my handbag spilled everywhere. A couple in a car stopped and picked them up, and two days later Mum received a letter that simply read, 'Handbag and contents found. Please contact this number.' Mum had already told the police that I was missing, so they rang the number. In the meantime someone had reported seeing me getting into a car with a man. The *East London Advertiser* picked up on the story and published a long article under the headline 'Girl Gone Missing', in which they reported the mystery of my belongings strewn across the motorway and the police's fears for my life. They even quoted Mick Garvey, who said, 'Please, Sharon, come home. We love you. We just want to know that you are safe. If you don't want to come home, we'll understand. But please, please let us know you are safe.'

When there was no response, and the police found no trace of me, Mum really did believe I was dead, and it broke her heart. I deeply regret being so careless with my bags, but I had no idea of the distress it would cause. Mick Garvey was no doubt secretly delighted at the prospect of my death: he didn't have me around to abuse, but on the other hand there was no longer any risk of me telling anyone about him.

The lorry driver pulled up at the first service station we came to and said, 'Let's get you a warm drink – you look frozen.'

We went into the café and I ordered fish, chips, peas, a slice of bread and a mug of tea. It tasted wonderful. Afterwards the driver said he was going to have a kip, and asked me to lie down with him in the bunk behind the front seats. I knew what was coming, but I didn't object. He'd been kind to me. I don't suppose it could be classed as rape, as I was over sixteen and did nothing to stop him, but he was certainly taking advantage of a vulnerable child. He was probably in his fifties, which to me seemed incredibly old, but I was beyond being repulsed. I had never valued my body, and it meant nothing to me. I had been given a meal and a lift, and the man was kind and polite, and said nice things to me. It was very different from my stepfather's aggressive sex. As usual, I went somewhere else in my head and just allowed it to take place. I'd never had a loving sexual relationship; to me, sex was just something men took from you. The concept of giving it, choosing to do it, was completely alien to me.

The driver dropped me at a service station near the M6 and gave me a couple of quid to get myself a hot drink. I stood in the car park at the service area, and this time I only approached lorry drivers who had the word 'Liverpool' on their vehicles. About the third one I spoke to said he would take me all the way. I had the nous to always tell everyone I hitched a lift from that someone was waiting for me at the other end; it was an instinct to protect my own safety. This lorry driver was a decent guy and had a picture of his wife and kids in the cab. I remember thinking, How nice – he's carrying his wife and kids with him everywhere. I knew Mick Garvey never carried pictures of us.

When I climbed out of his cab near the docks in Liverpool, I had no clear idea what to do. On impulse I walked into a police station, told them I was eighteen, though I was a year younger, and said I was looking for somewhere safe to stay. I gave a false name: Sherry, certainly, but I can't remember the surname. I used so many aliases over the next few months. They gave me the phone number of a hostel, and when I rang, there was fortunately a place available. The hostel was in Sydenham, just round the corner from Lark Lane, so I was a little bit worried that someone who knew my family would recognise me.

On the way there, I stole some scissors from a corner shop, went into the public toilets on Aigburth Road and hacked off my hair. I held my head over the sink, watched the long coils dropping in and told myself I was cutting Mick Garvey out of my life for ever. When I looked in the mirror, I was shocked and burst into tears. My hair had been shoulder length, but now it was above my ears and spiky. I tidied it as best I could, and once I got over the initial shock, I was happy to have so radically changed my appearance.

The hostel was run by a lovely couple, a black guy and his wife. At first I was suspicious of him, wondering whether he raped all the girls one by one, but I soon learned to trust them both. It was a girls-only hostel, and I made friends with some of the others, girls who, like me, had had tough lives. We used to sit around chatting over tea and toast, and one of the others helped me dye my hair. It was the height of the Sex Pistols' fame and I plastered my eyes with black kohl and gelled my purple, red and blue hair into spikes, partly because it was the fashion, but mainly because I was still worried about being recognised.

I stayed there for several months. I was there when Elvis Presley died, in August 1977. I can remember one of the girls saying that the King was dead.

'What king? We don't have a king, we have a queen,' I said ingenuously. But then I saw the headline in the newspaper and realised it was Elvis. I cried buckets for him, and for myself; it was as if his death had unleashed a great spring of self-pity in me, and for a couple of days I was very down.

I can't remember how the system at the hostel worked, because I wasn't able to claim benefits in my phoney name, but they provided me with food and lodgings, and also gave me a small amount of pocket money each week.

I saw a lot of Donna during these months, although we had to be very careful not to alert her mother or anyone else who knew my mum. The first time I rang her home, I put on a different voice when her mother answered, and when Donna came on the line I said, 'Don't say nothing but it's me, Sharon.'

We met almost every day after that. She'd walk round to Sydenham Avenue, and then we'd wander around the town together, or sit at the hostel smoking. The hostel ran work training programmes, but I couldn't go on any of them because I didn't have a National Insurance number. I think the warden thought I was lazy, but it was because I couldn't risk my real identity being discovered. I didn't want Mick to track me down, or the police as I'd absconded during my suspended sentence.

After I'd been there for three or four weeks, Donna told me worriedly, 'Your mum's been on the phone. She's really upset. The police are looking for you.'

'I don't care. There's no way I'm going back now. I'm a different person. Sharon no longer exists.'

It was at this time that Donna tried to broach the subject with her mother, Margaret, of me being abused. Margaret told her not to get involved: 'Sharon's been in a lot of trouble, running away all the time and getting involved with the police. She may be lying. Don't tell anybody. It could cause a great deal of trouble.'

I don't blame her: for all Margaret knew, I was the liar that Mick Garvey had always made me out to be. But it was yet another possible lifeline that had been snatched away from me.

One day I answered the door at the hostel to a policeman. The guy who ran the place was out with his wife collecting supplies, and there were only a few of the residents there.

'Have you seen this girl?' the copper asked, showing me a newspaper clipping with my face on it.

I looked at it, my heart pounding, but also curious to know why I was in the newspaper. I saw the headline 'Girl Gone Missing'. From my earliest days I had schooled myself to think on my feet and never panic, so after a second or two studying the page, I coolly looked up and met the policeman's eye and said, 'There's no one like that here, mate.'

Thanks to my punk-rock hair and lashings of face paint, he didn't recognise me. Mercifully, he left straight away, before any of the other girls came to see what was happening.

Thank you, God, thank you. I've been saved again, I thought.

But the encounter threw me: if he'd come two hours earlier, I'd have answered the door with a towel round my head and no make-up on, and he'd have recognised me. Now I was thinking, What if he comes back and someone else sees the picture? They'll tell him it's Sherry without her make-up on. Why is it that every time I feel safe, someone takes it away?

I knew I had to run away and not leave any trace. I couldn't risk even telling Donna. I had felt stable and secure at the hostel, and it had given me time to take stock of my life and relax. But once again I was moving on. I felt so sad that I had to leave – whatever I did, my past always seemed to catch up with me.

It was the end of November when I moved out, and the weather was turning cold. For three weeks I lived rough, eating in supermarkets, sleeping on the streets, helping myself to fresh clothes off washing lines. I spent my days wandering around the city centre, mooching about in shops and department stores to get warm. I went into an Oxfam shop and took three coats into the changing room, then spent ages stuffing the biggest and warmest into my small bag. I sauntered out and hung the other two back on the rail. Nobody noticed, and I figured someone had given the coat to charity in the first place. I was just a different charity.

At night I kept away from the streets, finding corners in back yards, and sometimes sitting in the small outdoor toilets that some houses still had. I washed in supermarket toilets, where the soap was so much nicer than in public lavatories.

It was a desperate, lonely, cold, miserable time. Every day passed in a blur of trying to keep warm and find food. When you are reduced to that very basic way of life, survival is all that matters. I scavenged like an animal, eating food off other people's discarded plates in cafés, looking in bins behind supermarkets, lurking in doorways to feel the warmth from the buildings. Often cars would pull up. 'Are you doing business, love?' the driver would ask.

'No. I'm meeting my dad just up the road,' I would reply. I did think about earning some quick and easy money, but I just couldn't bring myself to do it.

As Christmas approached, my life seemed very bleak. The city was covered in twinkling lights, there were happy crowds of shoppers jostling along the busy pavements, and Christmas music sounded from every shop. Everyone seemed to have somewhere to go and something to do. I thought about Mum and my brothers, then remembered that their Christmas would be happier because I wasn't there.

I had never felt more alone, more of an outsider.

CHAPTER ELEVEN

Three days before Christmas I heard about another hostel, near Chinatown. It was a filthy place, catering mostly for drug addicts, alcoholics and prostitutes. I checked in and was told the rules: out of the building by 9.30 a.m., a maximum of five nights' stay, no food or drink in the bedrooms. It was a disgusting, smelly place, but at least I had a bed and a roof over me.

On Christmas Day I woke to the sound of church bells ringing, and from the window I could see people in their smartest clothes hurrying to worship. Unusually, we were allowed to stay in the hostel all day, and at one o'clock one of the staff banged on my door to tell me that Christmas dinner would be served at 3 p.m. I was very hungry, as there were no supermarkets open to steal from, so I made my way to the dining hall for the meal. But I couldn't eat it. All around me were old men and women, many of them with no teeth, slurping and smacking their gums. There was a pervading smell of sweat and urine. I wanted to throw up. One of the helpers noticed I wasn't eating, and I asked if I could take my dinner somewhere else to eat it, but they said it was against the rules. So I left and went back to my room, hungry.

It was the first time I had been totally alone at Christmas, with no cards, no presents, no food. I cried and cried. It wasn't like me to feel self-pitying, but I was absolutely desperate. I thought, I'm seventeen, another year has passed, and it's not getting better. What do I have to do to have a good life?

I was crying because I missed Mum, Tom and Phil, because I was hungry on the one day of the year everyone was stuffing themselves, because I could see no future. I wasn't tempted to go home – nothing would take me back to Mick Garvey – but I missed Mum's cooking, and the family feeling of Christmas. I didn't think Mum or my real dad would be missing me; I was convinced they would be glad to be rid of me, because wherever I was I seemed to cause arguments.

I resolved to disappear again, running away from myself more than from anyone else. It may sound strange, but I decided to live on the motorways. I found it easy to get lifts, and inside the cab of a lorry I felt warm and safe. I knew I might occasionally have to trade sex in return for meals and lifts, but it was the kind of anonymous life I craved.

The day after Boxing Day I picked up a lift just outside the docks. The driver said he was going to Leeds, and I said I was too, as if it was a coincidence, to visit my sister, who was expecting me. He dropped me at the motorway exit near Leeds, and shortly afterwards I was in another lorry, travelling to Scotland.

I travelled the motorways for several months, going all over Britain. Sometimes I'd walk around the towns and cities I was dropped in; other times I would simply hitch my next ride and carry on. I never went hungry, because all the drivers were happy to buy me meals. Most of them were decent and didn't take advantage of me, but it did happen now and again, always when I was travelling at night. I never objected, and would keep my head separate from my body, as I had learned to do for years. The sex was never violent, never as horrible as anything Mick Garvey had done to me.

I lost track of time, not allowing myself to think about the past or the future, just living each day from morning to night, and hoping for somewhere warm to sleep and some food inside me. I had no plans, and I closed my mind to all my memories. I even missed my eighteenth birthday. When the news came on in a lorry cab and the announcer said it was 25 March, I let out a startled cry. When I explained to the driver that I'd missed my birthday by three days, he gave me a fiver. It was my only present, and he was a good man who wanted nothing in return.

Often the drivers wanted to talk: they had lonely jobs. But they were happy to let me sleep, which meant that if I did have to spend a few hours in a town or city, I was alert enough to look after myself. I felt very alone, and in my sorrow I can remember thinking, If this lorry crashes and I'm killed, nobody will ever know who I was or where I came from. I'll be buried in an unmarked grave.

It was as if my birth and my life had all been for nothing. I didn't know where to go, or what was expected from me, or even who I was. I didn't feel like a Costain, but I certainly wasn't a Garvey. The only name I really felt attached to was Luby, my mum's maiden name and the name of my grandparents and my beloved uncle Gordon. Thinking about them gave me a sense of having roots. But there was no way I could ever go back to my roots: I had to find my own way to survive.

For those months on the lorries I had no plans, no structure to my life, no routine, no regular mealtimes or sleep times, no limitations. I owned nothing except a few clothes. I had no papers or any identification. I didn't exist. But it couldn't go on for ever. It was as if I had, for a short time, put my brain on hold, to give it a rest. Eventually, though, I had to shake off my torpor and get a grip on my life.

One of the lorries dropped me in Glasgow at about five o'clock one morning, and I was standing by the side of the road looking over the parapet of a bridge at the dark waters of a river churning below. I thought about jumping, but then I told myself firmly, You're always planning suicide, but you never do it. Either do it now or put it right out of your mind and get on with what you've got.

I looked again at the water and it was too cold, dirty and dark to contemplate, so I walked away with a new sense of purpose. It would be too easy just to hitch another lift; I was going to do something else. Anything else. Unbeknown to me, an unlikely saviour was about to come into my life and help me turn everything round.

I stopped in a doorway to get out of the wind for a few minutes, then noticed the name on a brass plate: it was a hotel. On impulse I pushed it open. There was a flight of stairs leading up to the hotel lobby, and I was tempted to stay at the bottom of the stairs until I was warm, then move on. But no, I had decided to change my life, and this meant I must do something. The police would never look for me in Glasgow, as I had no connections there.

I went up to the hotel lobby, where a woman on the reception desk looked me up and down and raised her pinched nose in the air as if there was a smell under it. She was wearing a severe suit, her hair was pulled back tightly, and there were silver-rimmed glasses on her nose. We disliked each other on sight, but instead of intimidating me, she simply made me more determined.

'Can I see the manager, please?'

'What about?' she asked superciliously.

'A job,' I replied simply.

'We don't have any jobs.'

'I need to see the manager,' I insisted. 'It's very important. You're not fobbing me off.'

'Hold on.' With a resigned sigh she went into a small office behind the desk.

I could hear murmured voices, and then a man appeared. He was small, fat, Jewish and, to me, elderly. He looked at me keenly, and I asked if I could talk to him in private. I didn't want the harridan behind the reception desk listening. He acquiesced and ushered me into his office.

Once there, I said, 'I'm going to be honest with you. I have nowhere to live, I am on the streets, I am eighteen, and I have no job, no money, no food. If I don't do something about it today, I am going to kill myself. I'm not a drug addict, I don't drink, and I can work very hard. Can you give me a job? I don't want wages – all I'm asking for is a bed and some food. I'll work all the hours you give me.'

He paused and said, 'You really are desperate, aren't you? Stay here.'

He went out of the room, and I immediately worried that he had gone to call the police. After a few minutes panic started to set in and I was about to walk out when he returned.

'I'm happy to give you a chance,' he said, smiling.

He took me to the kitchens and paired me with another girl of about the same age. He told her to take me to my room and to find a uniform for me. To me he said, 'I want you to have a bath, wash your hair, and come back down to the kitchen for a meal. Today you will be shown the ropes. You start work tomorrow.'

I wrapped my arms round his neck and cried. The girl was looking at me as if I was a loony toon, but I didn't care. That little man had thrown me a lifeline, and I made sure I didn't mess it up. I did exactly what I had promised: I worked hard and uncomplainingly.

After my first week in the kitchens I became a chambermaid and a waitress. I didn't get too close to any of the other staff, with their constant bickering and alliances; I simply enjoyed the luxury of a bath every day, clean hair and my cosy, tiny attic bedroom. I was Sherry to everyone, and I really felt that Sharon was dead. I didn't have to give a surname, as there was no paperwork attached to my job. I was paid £15 a week in cash, which I'm sure was as good a deal for the hotel as it was for me.

I spent nothing; even the bath oils and the shampoos were from the chambermaids' trolleys. I didn't socialise, and when I wasn't working, I slept. Every penny I earned I put away. The tight-lipped woman on reception continued to make my life as difficult as possible, as she felt I had gone over her head to get the job. She'd always make sure I was on the worst shifts and find something to complain about. But what people like that never realise is that, in small ways like that, I am untouchable. Petty treatment by her meant nothing to me. If I could put up with Mick Garvey, I could put up with anything.

The hotel was a turning point in my life. I could have ended up in real trouble. Looking back, I can see the risks I took living on the streets and my blood runs cold. I got through by good luck and a certain amount of natural savvy, but it could so easily have gone horribly wrong.

The hotel, however, was only a stepping stone, and I was determined to keep moving upwards. After five months I had saved enough money to move into a bedsit, which cost £100 a month and required £100 deposit. I took a job in a pub, working 10 a.m. to 11 p.m. with a break during the day, six days a week. I was willing to work such unsociable hours because I had nothing else to do. On Sundays, my day off, I started going to church again and walked to the nearest one to my flat. I thanked God for seeing me through such a bleak time. I also established a routine of going for a walk and then cooking a proper Sunday dinner for myself.

The only real problem left from my old life was my inability to sleep. Those years of forcing myself to stay awake, waiting for Mick Garvey, had left me with a sleep problem that has dogged me all my life. I still sleep in snatches, in the early hours of the morning, and nightmares wake me up. So although I felt completely safe in my cosy bedsit, I would watch the hours of the night tick by, unable to sleep.

It was a lonely, isolated life, but I still wasn't prepared to trust anyone. At work, I was a classic bubbly barmaid, quick with the backchat to all the men I served, but I never allowed anyone to get close to me, even though some of them tried. I was always friendly, but I knew how to control anyone who was getting out of order, either with me or with other customers. The boss trusted me to run the pub on my own. I felt I had everything I wanted: a regular life, fashionable clothes and even, at last, a decent haircut – the sister-in-law of one of the pub regulars came to my flat and styled my hair into a bob.

I looked in the mirror and thought, I like this Sherry. She's lovely. She brings me luck.

And there was more good fortune to come. To my great surprise, I fell head over heels in love at first sight. A group of guys, all students, came into the bar, and the minute I clapped eyes on one of them it was that corny old thing, a real bolt from the blue. I felt my nerve endings tingle, and for the very first time in my adult life I looked at a man and wanted, more than anything, to get to know him.

I didn't know his name, but I was quick-witted and when he came to the bar to buy a round, I said, 'Sorry, love, I can't serve you – you're too young.'

He turned to his mates and told them what I'd said, and they all laughed. He said to me, 'I've got some ID.'

Then it was my turn to laugh and I said, 'I'm only fooling.'

That opened the door and we started chatting. He was a Glaswegian, Les Allan, just a year older than me and studying mechanical engineering at college. He asked if he could wait until closing time and then walk me home, and I was more than happy to agree. I spent the rest of the evening looking across at him, catching his eye as he glanced at me and feeling a deep surge of desire in the pit of my stomach.

Les and I were soon an item, and he'd wait for me every evening and walk me back to the bedsit. He lived at home with his parents, but he'd spend all his spare time with me. Les was the first person I felt I could be totally honest with, and I told him the story of my life. He knew that my name was really Sharon. He knew all about the abuse and my life on the streets. I wanted to give him the opportunity to walk away before we got in too deep. I had always felt that nobody would want me if they knew the full story, but I also wasn't prepared to snatch happiness under false pretences.

The fact that Les didn't care about my past made me love him even more. He boosted my self-esteem more than he ever realised. It was fantastic for me to discover that I wasn't worthless.

When I eventually felt ready to have sex, it was amazing. He was very gentle because he realised how difficult it must be for me. I was terrified that I wouldn't be able to go through with it, but I was also determined to try, because I wanted more than anything to be normal, and I really loved him. We did it in the dark, because I was still disgusted with my own body. He held me tenderly in his arms, stroked my face and made sure everything we did was by mutual consent. For the first time in my life I took part in it, and for the first time ever I had real choice. Although I loved Les and had strong sexual emotions, one of the most precious moments was when I said I didn't want to have sex right then and he accepted it.

I can choose! I thought to myself, amazed. I can say no and he respects it.

I never associated sex with Les with anything that Mick

Garvey had done to me. This was *making love*, and it was a completely different thing. My stepfather used power and violence; with Les, it was an emotional union, two of us in it together, and mad about each other. I had never experienced such freedom before. These were blissful days, and I couldn't remember any happiness like this since the day my stepfather came into my life.

Les and I soon felt very serious about each other, and the day came when he had to introduce me to his parents. I was dreading it: I knew they were a well-established middle-class family. His father was a very senior policeman. What would they make of me, a waif with a Liverpudlian accent, who worked as a barmaid? I dressed in my smartest clothes and made sure my hair was tidy.

Les's mother was perfectly polite and made sandwiches and tea, and later we were joined by his father, who also treated me with strained politeness. I think his parents put up with me for his sake, but all the time they were hoping we would split up and he would move on to someone more suitable.

Les faced a series of heated arguments with his family about being with me, which only pushed us closer together and made sure that we moved in together as soon as possible. We both felt we wanted to be together for ever. We were madly in love. He continued with his college course, and I worked to support us. We moved to a bigger bedsit and I can remember sitting on the windowsill watching him walk home up the road. I would play our favourite record, 'Three Times a Lady', at loud volume as the sun streamed in and my man walked towards me. I felt buckets full of love for him.

We spent Christmas that year with his family, and we all tried to get on, but it was simply a clash of two cultures. They accepted me because they didn't want to lose him, but it was clear that they weren't happy.

Away from his family, life with Les was perfect, and he was so accepting of my past that I began to pine for my family. For the first time in many months I started to feel that I could see them again. I had always longed to see Mum, Tom and Phil, but felt that I would bring trouble in my wake if I contacted them when Mick Garvey was still on the scene. I also knew that if I walked back, alone, into my bedroom at Ackroyd Drive, he would pick up where he had left off.

But now everything was different. I had my own man. I had Les.

Chapter Twelve

It took several attempts before I made contact with Mum. I would walk into a phone box and dial all the numbers except the last digit, then my nerve would fail and I would walk out. A day or two later I would try again and the same thing would happen. She won't want to talk to me, I'd tell myself as I hung up. She's glad I'm not around.

Sometimes I would even talk to the dialling tone, going through what I would say to her. I was also worried that somehow my old life would pollute my new. You've got a lot going for you now, I'd think. Why do you want to spoil it all? Mick Garvey will ruin your life again, one way or another. Why risk it?

But the urge to find out if Mum and my brothers were all right was too strong, and one day I finally managed to dial the whole number. I nearly panicked as I heard it ringing, but before I could run away it was picked up.

'Hello?'

Mum sounded exactly the same as she had always done. My heart leaped with joy.

'Hello, Mum. It's me, Sharon.'

There was silence on the other end of the line. I didn't realise that to her I was a voice from the grave. I had been missing for nearly two years, and after trying everything she could think of to find me, she had finally accepted that I was dead. My possessions strewn across the motorway had left little room for hope, and she was sure I had been murdered and buried somewhere.

It took her a few seconds to recover from the shock, but she was overjoyed to hear me and kept repeating my name over and over.

'Oh, my God!' she gasped, her voice trembling. 'Is it really you, Sharon? I'm not dreaming, am I? Sharon?' Then she burst into tears, and so did I. I was crying from the sheer joy of hearing her voice and knowing she was safe.

There was such a lot to catch up on, but the best news by far was that she was no longer with Mick Garvey. They had finally got married, but then soon afterwards they had split up. After the thrill of hearing he was off the scene, all I wanted to know about was Phil. Had Mick Garvey taken him? Thank God the answer was no. It felt like all my Christmases and birthdays rolled in one: my family was safe and well.

I had so many questions. Immediately I made up my mind to go home: the need to see them again was a physical ache. All the feelings and thoughts about them that I had suppressed during the time I had been on my own came flooding back. I was tired of pretending I belonged to nobody. While I was living rough or trying to build my own life, I had pushed away any memories of my past life because that way I didn't live with the questions: why didn't I tell them? Why didn't they save me? Why didn't anyone realise what I was going through?

Almost as soon as I put the phone down I told Les that I wanted to go and live in London. He had finished his college course by then and was happy to move with me. We were young and free, and we hitchhiked down. It was a strange feeling, being back on the motorways in the cabs of lorries, but it felt so different to be travelling with someone I cared about.

We made our way to Ackroyd Drive, where Mum hugged and hugged me. But the strange thing was that she didn't ask anything about the past. If it had been my daughter who had been away for two years, I'd want to know where she had been, why she hadn't made contact, what had made her go. But Mum's attitude was 'You're back now, so we'll start afresh.'

She liked Les, but she never wondered how I came to be in Glasgow to meet him. Perhaps she sensed that the answers would be too sad for her to bear. And for my part I asked no questions about her marriage to Mick Garvey or their split: I couldn't stand to hear his name mentioned.

Tom had turned into a young man while I was away. He was always out doing his own thing. Phil had grown the most; he was now twelve years old, at secondary school, just becoming an adolescent. There was an awkwardness between us all. I'd lost two years and they could never be replaced. Our closeness had gone, and it would take us some time to rebuild it.

Mum was the happiest I had seen her in a long time. She was still working in the pub and doing her own catering service, but she was more relaxed, less worried. My brothers, too, were enjoying the peace of not having Mick around; for years they had seen him beating up their mother, and it must have been very hard on them.

Les and I moved back into my old bedroom, and together we dispelled all the old, terrible memories. I still heard the floorboards creaking, and I refused to close the door tight so that I wouldn't see the handle turn, but I had learned how to put my fears away in boxes in my head. I'd tell myself, over and over, Don't let the past spoil the present, or you will be left with nothing.

I still had nightmares, but they were less frequent, and Les would hold me and whisper, 'It's all right. He's not here. I'm here. I'll take care of you.'

Mum would have been happy for us to stay there for ever, but we wanted our own place. We went to the council and, in a move that would astonish young couples today who have to sit for years on long waiting lists, we were given a set of keys that day to look at a flat on the Isle of Dogs. We were thrilled, and accepted it straight away. It was within walking distance of Mum, on the second floor of a small block of flats. There were two bedrooms, and a balcony at the front and back.

We moved in with nothing except a mattress, but all Mum's friends rallied round and gave us things. For a few weeks I had to cook on a camping stove with bottled gas, but then we were given a social security loan, which provided all the basics. Phil loved coming to stay with us.

Les found a part-time job, and I started to look for work, but our plans changed when I discovered I was pregnant. We were both thrilled; we hadn't planned the baby, which was due around the time of my twentieth birthday, but we'd talked about wanting children, and we were happy to start a family.

Unfortunately we needed to find somewhere else to live. The flat we had been so delighted with had become a real problem: the block was infested with rats. I was bitten by one, which was on the landing outside our door. When I opened the door, it must have felt threatened and bit my ankle before scampering away. I screamed in pain and shock. I had to go to hospital for tests to check that it hadn't infected me with any nasty disease.

We and all our neighbours pleaded with the council to close the block and rehouse everyone, but our demands fell on deaf ears. In desperation, a band of about twenty of us marched to Downing Street and actually camped there overnight before handing in a petition. Nowadays Downing Street is closed to protesters, but back in 1979 we were able to pitch our sleeping bags across the street from Number Ten. We held banners, and the police put a metal barrier in front of us. Reporters and television cameras came down to record our protest. Because I was pregnant and had been bitten by a rat, and also because I am happy to speak out when I feel strongly, I was pushed forward to do the interview.

When we got home after handing in the petition, I switched on the television and there I was, on the one o'clock news. It was quite a surprise to see myself. The protest worked, because within days Les and I were rehoused to a maisonette in St Paul's Way, five minutes from Mum. She was thrilled at having us so close, and even more thrilled at having a grandchild on the way. But there was one thing she was determined to do.

I was sitting at home watching *Coronation Street* one evening when she arrived, with her friend Eileen and a large box.

'You know what's in the box, don't you?' she asked.

'No.'

She opened the lid and there was a traditional white wedding dress. 'If that baby's coming, you want to get married. I've been to see the vicar.'

I was astonished. 'I don't want to get married, Mum.'

Les had asked me twice, and twice I had turned him down. Not because I didn't love him, but it simply wasn't in my make-up to tie myself down. I didn't want to lose the independence I had spent so long building up. Also, it didn't seem ideal to wear a white dress in church when I was three months pregnant. But Mum, and everyone else, was so disappointed that I felt I was taking her pleasure away, and more than anything I wanted to please her. So I agreed to it, and the wedding was set for 19 September 1979.

Les's family was in for a double shock: he rang them one week to tell them I was pregnant, and then the following week to tell them about the wedding. I think they were gutted, as they had really hoped our affair would blow over. But they made the best of it and agreed to come to the wedding.

I asked my uncle Gordon to give me away. He was the most dependable male figure in my life, someone I knew loved and cared for me. He was so pleased to say yes. Mum busied herself with all the arrangements, hiring a hall, booking a gold Rolls-Royce and choosing flowers. She did the catering herself, of course, and arranged a magnificent spread.

How can I describe the wedding day? I'm not sure that there are words in my vocabulary. 'Horrendous' is a good start, but it was even worse than that. I was getting married from Mum's home, so I spent the night before the wedding in my old bed in my old room without Les. I lay awake, remembering my past and thinking, I don't want to get married. It's all right now, but what will it be like in five years' time? Why do we have to go through with this?

All the fears and problems of my childhood seemed to close in on me again. I was worried that I was not a fit person to marry, worried that I would make a mess of my life and then worried that I was thinking like this. Most of all, I had a terrible feeling that my happiness was under threat, that my contented life, which I had worked so hard to create, was about to come crashing down around me. I had a very strong feeling of impending doom, and all the old anxiety began to gnaw at my stomach.

I spent a terrible, sleepless night, and the next morning, as Mum and her friend Doreen did my hair and make-up in my bedroom, I said firmly, 'I'm not getting married.'

'Yes you bloody are,' Mum said. 'You've just had an attack of the wobblies, that's all,' she said, before bustling off downstairs.

I sighed, knowing that there was little point in arguing. I looked around. Uncle Gordon was there, looking wonderful in his suit, and I was beginning to enjoy the preparations.

Looking at myself in the mirror, I really did look like a princess in my long white gown and with flowers in my hair. I didn't have a pregnancy bulge yet, but I had the softened, glowing looks of an expectant mother.

My reverie in front of the mirror was cut short by shouting downstairs. Mum rushed back into the bedroom, grim-faced and with tears on her cheeks. 'You are going to have to go through with it – there'll be murder if you don't,' she stuttered, panic in her eyes.

'What?'

'He's down there.'

'Who?' I asked, totally bewildered.

'Mick. And he's going to give you away.'

My stomach lurched and for a moment I thought I was about to be sick. Just like that Mick Garvey was going to ruin my special day. 'No he's not,' I said, when I'd caught my breath. 'I want Gordon to give me away.'

'Please, Sharon. If you don't let him, he'll destroy every-thing. It's not just your wedding, he'll destroy *everything*. There's going to be murder, I mean it.'

I could tell from her face how upset she was. I, too, was devastated. It was the worst thing I could have wished for, but it instantly explained all my fears of the previous night. This was what my premonition of disaster was about. I knew that I faced a choice: I either let him give me away or he would screw up the whole day. Gordon was deeply disappointed, and I was beside myself. Even though I didn't want to get married, I didn't want him spoiling everything. It seemed like a terrible black omen, and I realised that the night before, when I had panicked, I had been fighting off the foreboding that in some way this man, who had done everything possible to ruin my past, would come back to darken my future.

When I walked downstairs in all my finery and saw Mick

standing in the hallway, I felt physically sick. He looked ridiculous, wearing a white suit and a black shirt open at the neck. I pulled down my veil when I saw him and refused to lift it. Even as the photographer tried to take pictures of us leaving the house and getting into the Rolls-Royce together, my veil was down.

Travelling with him to the church, he tried to talk to me, his usual leering talk: 'I bet you're looking forward to tonight, aren't you?'

The driver in front was a friend of his, so Mick couldn't say anything cruder, and he didn't try to touch me. I later discovered that Mick had heard about the wedding from this man.

I turned my head away and stared out of the window through my veil. I felt it was blasphemous him giving me away. I wanted to say to him, *How dare you go into a church? How can you face God?*

As we walked down the aisle, I refused to put my arm through his and he had to hold my elbow. I was so anxious to get away from him that halfway down he had to tell me to slow down. Before the altar, Les was waiting for me, with Tom beside him as the best man. I could tell from the look on their faces they knew what agony I was in. A phone call had told them what had happened. I felt so offended that my stepfather was giving me away to Les, as if he was giving permission for Les to have his cherished daughter. It made me feel dirty again, and that was a feeling I had managed to slowly rid myself of over the past two and a half years.

When we were posing for the pictures after the ceremony, I said to Les, 'Don't worry about him. This is our day, not his.'

Les agreed, and was determined to make the best of it and not let his presence spoil the occasion.

Sadly, that was easier said than done. There were lots of

Mick's pals at the wedding: he had invited all his lowlife criminal friends, which didn't exactly go down well with my new in-laws. In fact, everything was spoiled. I stood at the doorway to the reception and looked at Mum's hard work: there was champagne, a beautiful three-tier wedding cake, whole glazed salmons and mounds of other, fantastic food that had cost her a lot of money and hours and hours of effort, and it was all tainted.

I put my hand on my swelling stomach and whispered a promise to my baby: 'This man will never affect your life. He is nothing to do with me, and nothing to do with you. I promise always to protect you.'

Inevitably, there was much animosity and many arguments among the guests, with the wannabe gangsters flashing their money around. Mick started an argument with my new father-in-law about who should put money behind the bar, and Les and I were on tenterhooks that the whole thing would erupt.

I spent an hour in the toilets crying, until Les persuaded me to come out. Mum kept apologising to me all day, as if it was her fault. Eventually I said to her, 'Don't blame yourself, Mum. But some day somebody has got to stand up to him.'

After the fiasco of the wedding I assumed that Mick Garvey had slipped away to whichever sewer he had suddenly appeared from, and I fervently hoped he would never again disrupt our family life.

One night when I was seven months pregnant Les, Tom and I spent the evening with Mum, who cooked us dinner. We left for home quite early because I was tired, but as we walked away, I realised I had left my keys at Mum's. I told Tom and Les I would catch them up. I was only five minutes away, so I was soon back in Ackroyd Drive. As I approached the house, I could hear screaming and breaking glass. I listened to the

familiar sounds of my childhood: a gruff voice barking obscen-
ities, Mum calling out for help, furniture smashing. I ran to the
window and could see Mick Garvey holding Mum down in a
chair. He was pointing into her face and yelling foul language
at her. I hammered on the door. He opened it and I pushed
past him and ran to her.

'What the hell are you doing letting this animal back in
your house?' I shouted. I didn't think about it: the anger just
erupted from me. I thought furiously, I'm not having him hit
my mother any more. He's not giving her a smacking for no
reason.

If I'd agonised about it, I'm sure the old fears would have
surfaced, but at that moment all I could think was that I
wanted him out of our lives.

'Who are you fucking talking about?' he growled.

'I'm talking about you,' I shouted, squaring up to him. 'I'm
not frightened of you. All right?' I picked up my keys and
turned back to my mum, aware of the adrenaline pumping
through my veins. 'Right, Mother, I'm off. If he comes near
this house again and you let him in, you have yourself to
blame.' I said it very coolly. My strength was totally
unexpected, as if some outside force had consumed me. I felt
no fear, and I wanted him to see that I was no longer in his
power, and nor was my mum.

As I walked down the path, I could hear him following me.
I thought, He's going to punch me in the back of the head, but
I'm not going to let him. I'm in control here.

I turned to face him, aware out of the corner of my eye that
the neighbours were all watching. 'Come on, then, big man.
Hit me.'

Mum was screaming, 'No, no, don't hit her – she's
pregnant!'

I calmly said, 'Mum, don't worry. I'm not frightened of him

any more.' I was willing him to hit me; I wanted him to. God forgive me, but I wasn't considering the safety of my unborn child, I was thinking, If you hit a pregnant woman with the neighbours watching, you'll go to prison.

To him I said, 'I tell you what, do you want me to let the world know what you're really like?' and I gestured at the people who were watching.

He was jumping up and down with rage and hurling abuse at me: 'You slag, you bastard...'

I carried on steadily: 'Go away now and don't come back here. Go now or I will tell my mum and the whole world what Mick Garvey really is.'

Mum was shouting, 'Leave him, leave him – you know what he's like.'

He stared at me, as if trying to work out whether I meant what I said. Then he turned abruptly and walked back into the house.

I felt elated, and no fear. Being a married woman with a child inside me and a happy life of my own had empowered me. It was a huge triumph: for the first time in my life I had stood up to him and won. He knew I was serious about telling everyone, and he was terrified of what I would say.

I said to Mum, 'I'm not coming back until you've got rid of him for good, and I mean for good. If that means you never see me again, or your grandchild, it's your choice. Get him out of your life!'

She did. As far as I know, that was the last time he went there.

I was on a high for a few days afterwards. I had fought a battle with my past and had emerged victorious. It felt unbelievably liberating.

Unfortunately, I couldn't rid myself of Mick Garvey that easily. When I went for an antenatal appointment, the gynaecologist who was examining me said gently, 'Excuse me, you don't have to answer if you don't want to, but have you ever been raped or abused?'

My breath caught in my throat. 'Yes,' I said quietly. 'How did you know?'

'There's a lot of scar tissue, caused by internal bruising and bleeding.'

It was another kick in the teeth. My stepfather had left me a permanent legacy: internal damage. The doctor told me I should be able to have my baby naturally, but if necessary I would have to have a Caesarean.

About a week before my twentieth birthday, in March 1980, I knew the birth was imminent. I found myself scrubbing the house from top to bottom, tidying all the cupboards, checking that I'd got everything I needed for the new arrival. It was the nesting instinct, and true enough, at four o'clock in the morning of 19 March labour started.

When Les told Mum I was having the baby, she rushed to the hospital to be with me. I have never felt closer to her than I did that day. I was in labour for another twelve hours – I can remember at one stage yelling at a nurse, 'Get it out or put it back! Just don't leave me like this!'

My beautiful son was born naturally that evening, three days before my twentieth birthday, and I felt the strongest surge of love I have ever felt in my life. A mother's love is the hardest bond to break, and mine was set like cement from that first moment. We'd decided on the name David for a boy before the birth, naming him after Les's brother. Phil wanted the baby to be named after him, so we gave him Philip as a second name. Mum came in as soon as David was born and burst into tears when she saw me lying there cuddling him.

'Here, Mum, hold your grandson.'

Tears streaming down her face, Mum cradled my new son.

I felt so moved by the thought that she had gone through everything I had just experienced in order to have me when she was barely sixteen. I felt love singing through my whole body for the baby in her arms, and for the woman holding him. And I felt a deep sense of pride in myself. I thought, I didn't take drugs. I didn't commit suicide. I didn't become a prostitute. I gave birth to this beautiful boy, and I'm going to make sure no harm comes to him.

Throughout everything I kept in touch with Donna. We would go for six months or more with no contact, but when we spoke it was as if we'd been in touch every day; there was never any awkwardness. We got married and had babies within months of each other. It was as if our lives were running on parallel tracks.

At the first opportunity, when David was three months old, I took him to Liverpool to see Donna and her daughter, Danielle. We had a wonderful reunion and spent hours catching up with all the details of our lives. We were so happy, pushing our babies together along the streets where we had played as urchins all those years earlier.

For the next year I was too busy, and happy with my baby, to pay much attention to my marriage, but I think both Les and I felt that the magic we'd had was slipping away. Mum was besotted with her grandson and was popping in twice a day, on her way to and from work. In the evenings if Mum was at home I'd often push the pram round to her house. Les was working full-time in a factory and was often not at home in the evenings.

When I found out I was pregnant again, I was delighted: I thought it might bring us closer together, and I was keen to have a baby brother or sister for David. But one evening when I was three and a half months pregnant, I collapsed bleeding in the bathroom as I was running a bath. There was an excruciating pain in my stomach. I banged frantically on the wall, hoping the woman next door would hear me, but when that failed I crawled downstairs, leaving a trail of blood, and fell in a heap on the doorstep, screaming for help.

An ambulance was called and little David was taken to Mum's. I spent a night in hospital, where I was told I had miscarried my baby. It was a bleak time: I felt deflated and empty, and desolate that I was going home with nothing to show for my pregnancy. For days I would burst into tears easily. Luckily, the demands of having to look after David, who was an energetic little chap, helped me through.

I did wonder whether the internal damage had caused me to lose my baby, but the medical staff kept reassuring me that it was something that could have happened to anyone, and that there was no reason why I should not get pregnant again.

As the months wore on, it was clear my marriage to Les was in trouble, but we both wanted to make it work, and we agreed on a completely fresh start. We'd been up to Scotland to visit his grandparents, who lived near Inverness, and we decided that we should move there. I wasn't willing to throw away my marriage without a fight. Whatever things were like between me and Les now, I could remember the true happiness we had had in the beginning, and I knew that my son had been conceived in great love. I wanted to give it another chance.

Mum was heartbroken we were moving so far away. She adored 'Dados', her little grandson. I felt I was ripping something away from her again, but I also felt it was necessary. We moved to a poky two-bedroom, freezing-cold cottage about two miles from the nearest main road, a difficult place to live without a car. It was such a shock after the bustle and noise of London. A trip to a shop involved a three-hour walk, and the weather was often rough. On fine days David and I had a beautiful playground: we were surrounded by fields set against a backdrop of mountains, and squirrels, rabbits, foxes and deer were often the only living things we saw until Les returned from work.

Things between Les and me improved, and I began to believe there was a chance for us, though I had become achingly lonely. A short while later I was thrilled to find I was pregnant again, the result of us clinging together against the cold in the cottage. Unfortunately, we had no phone and I felt completely isolated. After four months I was relieved to be offered a council house in the town of Inverness, and I revelled in the newfound civilisation of shops, a church, mother and baby groups, neighbours to talk to and a phone box to call Mum. Like her, I'm a good homemaker, and although we moved in with nothing, I very quickly acquired from second-hand shops everything we needed.

I had always wanted a playmate for David and felt that two children would make our family complete. We had a lovely house, with a garden front and back. I should have been very happy. Sadly, Les and I weren't getting on once again, and it was looking as though our fresh start was doomed.

CHAPTER THIRTEEN

My second baby made a dramatic entry into the world. I was shopping with a friend when my waters broke. It was a shock: nobody had warned me it could happen. Thinking I had peed, I was mortified. One of the shop staff offered to call a taxi, but I was foolhardy enough to decide to go by bus.

My friend asked the bus driver, 'How long to get to the hospital? She's in labour.'

The bus driver panicked and shouted out, 'We're going straight to the hospital. If you want to get off, get off now, because we're not stopping along the way. She's having a baby!'

I lay down on the back seat and I could feel the baby coming, much faster than David. Fortunately, we made it to the hospital, and I was whisked inside in a wheelchair.

We rang Les, and then I rang Mum. 'I'm having the baby. I'll phone you when it's over,' I said in a rush.

Half an hour later I gave birth to my second beautiful boy, with Les arriving five minutes before he did. There was none of the pain of my first labour, and Mum couldn't believe it when I phoned her straight away to tell her she had another grandson.

Sadly, although the birth was easy for me, our poor little son had to be rushed to the special care unit because he wasn't breathing properly. A minister was called in to baptise him and we had to agree a name straight away. I chose Gordon because I believed my uncle's name would give our precious child the strength he needed to pull through, which he did.

I missed my mum terribly in the next few weeks. I'd feared I might not love another baby as much as I loved David, but the minute Gordon arrived I knew that my capacity for love was infinite. I loved them differently, but completely and utterly.

Not long after Gordon's birth something wonderful happened for Mum. She went on holiday to Florida, and while she was there, she met a new man. This time her judgement was spot on: John Fenlon was a diamond, a really good, gentle, kind person who was so right for her. He came from London and was also on holiday out there. They joked that they had to travel across the Atlantic to meet and fall in love. They got engaged and married within two years. As Mum said, at their age there was no point wasting time when you knew you had found the one.

John worked as a manager for a haulage company, and by coincidence he had known Mick Garvey while working as a lorry driver years before. The whole family liked John, and he was generous with his money, which enabled Mum in turn to be generous with me.

Soon after they were married, Mum realised her lifelong ambition of buying a beach chalet at Clacton, with John, Mum and Tom each paying a third. She was thrilled, and we all had holidays there. She'd take my boys there for a couple of weeks in the summer, and I'd join them for the second week. Finally, after a lifetime of struggle, things had worked out well for Mum.

Sadly, this was not true for me and Les, and eventually we decided that the only way forward was to split up. It was a very difficult time, particularly as I was so far away from my family. Mum would send me money to get the train down to see her whenever she could afford it, and every couple of weeks a parcel would arrive full of clothes for the boys, pocket money for them, packets of soup and money for me. Without her, I suppose we would have survived, but it would certainly have been even harder than it was.

Living on benefits was very tight, and the next three years were difficult. I sank into a deep depression. The end of my marriage felt like another rejection for me, and I puzzled over how so much love and hope could have turned so sour. I couldn't work, because I became terrified at the thought that my children might be abused if I wasn't with them. The nightmares, which had become just an occasional feature during my happy times with Les, returned with a vengeance. I became frightened of sleep again, staying awake all night and snatching naps during the day when Gordon slept.

To be frank, I wasn't stable and had a lot of irrational thoughts. Suicide came back into my head on an endless loop, and if it hadn't been for the children, I'm sure I would have done it. I felt that I had worked so hard, against terrible odds, to become normal, to set up an ideal family with a mum and dad and two children, and it had all been dashed. I had done nothing wrong, but I felt it was my fault. Worse, I was still in love with Les.

Outwardly, I seemed all right. I have always been able to separate my inner turmoil from the Sharon I show to the world. My neighbours and friends came to me for advice and help, and I never said no. I always felt that if I did things for other people, someone would value me – because I didn't value myself. I spent miserable evenings alone when the children were in bed.

Monday was benefits day and I had to eke out the money carefully. I paid the bills and bought an electricity card, then purchased food and anything the children desperately needed, like new shoes. Some days I went without eating; at other times supper would be a plate of boiled potatoes. My neighbours were kind. There were lots of jobs in Inverness at that time and their husbands all worked, so they'd give me things. I climbed into the bath after the children, to make the most of the hot water, and if a letter or parcel arrived from Mum, I'd dance around the kitchen in delight.

After a bleak three years on my own I met a wonderful, caring man who changed my life in a very important way. James came into my world one evening when I had been looking after a friend's baby while she went out. When she came to collect him, there were three or four people with her, and they all came in for coffee. James and I hit it off straight away. He was a DJ, working in local clubs and hotels, and he looked like Don Johnson from *Miami Vice*, his dark hair streaked with blond. He was in his forties, and I was only twenty-six, but there never seemed to be an age gap.

The attraction was purely physical, although I came to like James very much. I'd been starved of love and affection for so long, and there was an instant sexual chemistry, which I was happy to act on. I was never in love with James, but our loving was sweet and frequent, and I felt renewed. He persuaded me to go out and enjoy myself. It was hard, at first, to trust anybody to babysit, but I did it. Most of all, James made me feel human again, a desirable woman.

We both knew it wasn't a serious or lasting relationship, but we enjoyed it for what it was, and it provided me with the confidence – and the push – that I needed for the next major step in my life.

My nightmares remained bad throughout this time, and they scared James. As with Les, I'd told him all about the abuse at the beginning of the relationship, giving him the opportunity to walk away if he wanted to. I was always convinced that when I told a man, he would find me dirty and not want to go near me, and I didn't want to be in a relationship under false pretences. The nightmares would wake James, as I thrashed about the bed moaning and screaming. Sometimes he'd get up in the morning and find I wasn't there, but curled up on the couch, or even asleep inside a cupboard. One night he followed me as I sleepwalked to the kitchen and began to take a knife out of a drawer. I was saying, 'I'm going to kill him,' over and over, clearly dreaming that I would kill Mick Garvey. James took the knife out of my hand, gently led me to the living room and wiped my face with a damp flannel to wake me.

Naturally, he was worried about what would have happened if he hadn't been there, and he told me that I needed to be honest with my mother about what had happened to me as a child. He felt sure that if I could tell my family, I would be able to come to terms with it better. I wasn't ready to face telling Mum, but eventually James forced my hand: 'If you don't phone or write to your mother and tell her, I promise you that on Monday I am going to phone her. You are suffering here, and nobody's helping you.'

I really didn't want Mum to hear about my abuse from anybody else. She didn't know James, and it would have been wrong if he had told her. So that night I started writing a letter. The first sentence was very hard, but once I had that down on paper, the rest came pouring out, and by the time I'd finished I'd filled ten pages.

The final page read:

> If you don't believe me, I will understand, because what woman wants to believe that her daughter was abused for all those years by someone she loved? But I've got no reason to lie. I am now a grown woman with children of my own, and I have no need to hurt you like

this if what I am saying is not true. And I don't want to hurt you, but I have been given no choice.

If you do believe me, ring me on Saturday at 10 a.m. If you don't ring, I will know you don't believe me, and you will never hear from me and my kids again, because I have to live with this, and I need someone to believe me and acknowledge that I have suffered and been abused.

I knew the letter would hurt her – just writing it devastated me, and I had lived with this truth all my life. For her, it would be a terrible shock. I posted the letter on Tuesday, giving it plenty of time to reach her before the weekend. Then I endured the terrible wait. I couldn't sleep, and huge battles were raging in my mind.

She's not going to call, said one voice inside my head.

Yes she is. She loves you, another replied.

If she loves me, why didn't she see what was going on?

How could she see? He was clever.

I tried to quell the conflicting thoughts, but the battle raged all week.

James was very supportive, and he even offered to be there with me when I walked to the callbox on Saturday, but I didn't want anybody there. I took the children, but I went prepared with sticks of Highland toffee to bribe them, and fortunately the callbox was next to a little park where they could play.

I was there fifteen minutes early, and there was a woman in the box. When she finished her call, I went and stood in there. Another woman asked if she could use the phone, but I explained I was waiting for a really important call. She was fine about it and kindly said she would go to the shops and phone from there.

So I waited and waited, for what seemed like an eternity.

CHAPTER FOURTEEN

Dead on 10 a.m. the phone rang.

'Hello, Mum?' I said timidly.

'Sharon, are you all right?' Mum asked, her voice flooded with concern.

I burst into tears. 'Mum, I'm so glad you phoned me.'

'Oh, Sharon, I believe you. I'm so sorry. How could I not see?'

'It was nothing to do with you, Mum. Don't blame yourself.'

We were both sobbing. For me, there was a huge sense of relief, like a heavy weight being lifted. Just to hear that phone ring, and to know she believed me, meant I felt I could cope with anything. I wasn't alone any more. I'd already told other people – Donna, my real dad, Les, James – but now I was telling one of the most important people in my world. Not only was she my mum, but she had been there through my childhood.

We were on the phone for an hour and a half. Thankfully it was the end of summer and nice weather, and the boys played happily. People came to use the phone and then walked away when they saw me sobbing. I poured my heart out. I didn't give Mum the details of what Mick Garvey had done to me, but I gave her scenarios, reminding her of all the times he had taken me upstairs to tidy my room, and the confrontation when I had been pregnant and had made him back down by threatening to let the world know about him.

I asked her tentatively, 'Do you blame me for what happened?' It was one of my greatest fears, that people who heard about the abuse would think I was part of it, that I had enjoyed it.

'How can I blame you?' she asked, shocked. 'You were a little child.'

She said she blamed herself for not realising what was going on, but I reassured her: 'You were a victim yourself. How can a victim save another victim, when they can't save themselves?'

She told me she hated him, and that having heard from me, she was finally able to put in place some pieces of the jigsaw. 'I don't like the picture,' she said, sighing, 'but at least I've got the picture. I always thought I was his victim, but now I know you were the worst victim.'

For the first time in my life I felt as though I was on a level with my mum, that we were equals, two women talking together. It made me feel privileged, and grateful that I had kept strong for all those years. I had finally got the acceptance I needed from the one person who mattered most, my mum. Only I knew how narrowly I had avoided becoming a prostitute, a drug addict, an alcoholic, a lunatic in an asylum – keeping myself safe and whole had finally paid off, and I felt clean again.

Mum told me she had showed my letter to Tom, and to a couple of her friends who knew Mick Garvey. She said, 'There are people looking for him. He's dead when they get their hands on him.'

In many ways, I'd rather Mum had gone to her grave without knowing, because the last thing I wanted was to cause her pain, but I needed to redress the balance. I had already caused her so much upset and suffering by running away, and I wanted her to know that it wasn't my fault, that my bad behaviour had come from him, not me.

She told me she was sending some money and wanted me to come for a break in London straight away.

That phone call was a matter of life and death for me: I'm not sure that I could have carried on had she not rung. She was the anchor of our family, and if the anchor chain had snapped away from me, I don't know if I would have coped for much longer.

The boys played on, oblivious to the high drama in the phone box. At the end of the call I beckoned them across to speak to their nan, and we finally said goodbye. I walked home a different person from the one who had made her way to the callbox in a tense and nervous state. I felt I was seeing the world for the first time in colour, not black and white.

Within days we made the long journey to London, and when Mum opened the door to us, she hugged me fiercely and told me how much she loved me. But the strangest thing was that the abuse was never mentioned the whole time I was there. When I tried to bring it up, she said, 'Sharon, you're here, you're safe, nothing bad is ever going to happen to you again.' It reminded me of what my real dad had said, when he was told. It was as if what had happened to me was so terrible that it was beyond words, beyond even thinking about. When I asked her if she truly believed me, she said, 'Of course I do, but I don't want you to be upset.'

I think she really meant that *she* didn't want to be upset. I didn't mind her reluctance to discuss it, although I would have welcomed the chance to talk it through. The acknowledgement was what I craved, and I had that. Tom didn't mention it either, but I felt very close to him. Phil was by now quite grown-up, and I took care not to allude to the abuse while he was around. Mum said that nobody knew where Mick Garvey had gone, that he had vanished off the face of the earth.

I took the children back to Inverness after our break, and

decided that it was time I left Scotland behind. But I didn't want to go to London; I wanted to go to my spiritual home, Liverpool. I wanted to be with people who talked like me, thought like me, shared my sense of humour. I had a strong feeling that the Scousers would see me through.

I put an advert in the *Liverpool Echo* for an exchange of council houses, and a family from Dovecot, near Huyton, came to see me. They had relatives in Inverness and were happy to move into my place. Dovecot wasn't an area I knew, but I felt it would be a foot into Liverpool, and when I rang Donna and Uncle Gordon, they said it was a decent area. So, sight unseen, I accepted the exchange. I was sad to part from James, but we both knew that our relationship wasn't for ever.

Just a short while later I was delighted to find myself back in Liverpool. The house was fine, but unfortunately I didn't fit into the neighbourhood. It was just too far from the parts of the city I knew and felt comfortable with, and although I usually find it easy to make friends, I didn't seem to fit in there.

Eventually I was so desperate to get back to the Lark Lane area that I gave up my council tenancy and rented a flat privately, in Parkfield Road. My life had come full circle: this was the road where Mum and Dad had lived when I'd cut my hand on the rose bush as a baby. It was a lovely flat in a huge Victorian house, with views across Princes Park and a bedroom each for the boys, who now went to the same primary school that I had attended as a child. It all felt good.

Although telling Mum had helped me deal with my memories of abuse, I was still very disturbed by them. I found more peace moving back to my favourite area. I had always believed a time would come when I would bring Mick Garvey to account for what he had done to me, but I hadn't formulated a plan, just a vague conviction that what goes around comes around. I felt it most strongly when walking along Lark Lane, past the police station, and the dry-cleaner's where Mum used to work. I could imagine her standing there. Donna was now very much back in my life. We'd link arms walking to the shops as if we were eight years old again. She, too, had a second child, Lewis. Our lives were still mirroring each other's.

I'd had no contact with my dad since I'd walked out of his flat thirteen years earlier, but one day, when I was twenty-nine, I was reading the *Liverpool Echo* and saw a story about a girl called Patricia Costain, who was one of three children who had fallen through a roof and had a narrow escape. Her father, Edward Costain, was quoted as saying how lucky they had been. I instantly knew this was my dad, and that Patricia was a half-sister I had never met or even heard of. From the exert I felt an instant bond with her.

The article gave the name of the road where they lived but not the number. I wasted no time: I jumped into a cab and went round there. When I reached the right road, I paid the driver and asked a woman passing by if she knew where Eddie Costain lived.

'Right here,' she said. 'You're standing next to his gate.'

I went to the door and it was opened by Margie. She and dad had split up, but she was round visiting him. She knew me as soon as she saw me, and all three of us were delighted to be reunited. Dad looked older and smaller. We cried as we hugged, and from then on we kept in contact, seeing each other every few weeks.

Outwardly, as ever, I seemed content. But when the door to my flat closed in the evenings, and the children were in bed, I was haunted by my past, and by my inability to come to terms with who I really was. I was at times manic, displacing all my fears and anxieties in frantic bursts of cleaning and cooking, staying up all night to fight off the demons that came to me in sleep.

Donna was the only one who had a clue about how I felt. She listened, she never judged me, and she was always there for me.

I visited Mum, but I felt that to be with the family I loved I had to relive memories of the abuse. When I stayed with her, I had to sleep in the room where he had crept in to rape me so many times, and now I didn't have a husband to hold me and protect me from my past. My only real refuge was with Uncle Gordon and Auntie Anne. With them, and their three wonderful sons, I felt at peace, completely free from the past. Gordon told me, years later, that when he'd first heard about the abuse he hadn't believe it: he thought I was trying to get back at Mick Garvey for the terrible childhood he had inflicted on us. I admired his honesty in telling me. When eventually he heard the full story, he totally accepted what I said.

I spent a lot of weekends with Gordon and his family, and at other times they would offer to have my sons, David and Gordon, for a couple of days, to give me a break. I owe a great deal to them – they helped me hold on to my precarious sanity.

As part of my fresh start in Liverpool I had enrolled at Knowsley Tertiary College, doing a course in Media and Communications, and this was a huge help, as I enjoyed stretching my mind. I relished getting back into education, which was something else my brutal stepfather had taken from me. But the college also helped in another way: it introduced me to a new man.

While at the college I heard of a writer's workshop in Page Moss and there I met John Carter who was a student at Liverpool University. I was still writing poetry, and at this stage I was also working on the script of a play and wanted to find a writers' workshop to help me with it. In the canteen at Page Moss writer's workshop, John invited me along to the Limelight club, another place where writers met. I hadn't thought about him romantically until that moment, but when my eyes met his, I fell in love.

John had been separated from his wife for seven months and had three children. He was about four years older than me, tall, good-looking, going bald. I was attracted to him and discovered that we had a lot in common; we soon began spending a lot of time together, often going to the cinema and theatre.

The play I was writing was about my abuse: I wanted people to know that it is possible to survive it and it doesn't have to destroy you. It is painful, and you have no control over the flashbacks, but you can develop your own survival techniques, as I did. I also wanted the play to open the eyes of people in authority who dealt with abused children – the police, social workers, teachers and doctors. Sexual and physical abuse were, for the first time, on the national agenda in a big way, with the launch of Childline in 1986, and I felt I had a great deal to contribute to a better understanding of it.

I took my play to a drama group, and with their help it was staged at the Eleanor Rathbone Theatre, part of Liverpool University. I wrote it, produced it, took the main role and directed it, but with some input from a professional director. I called the abused woman Melanie, but apart from that it was autobiographical. The play was called *Mental/Physical*, like my poem. The person who played the abuser, a really nice guy called Ian, was very upset by it, and it really drew on his resources as an actor.

There were about eight of us in the cast, and the rest, although amateurs, were used to appearing on stage. For me, it was completely new, and I'll never forget the moment the curtains opened on the first night. I was sitting on the stage in school uniform, and the sight of the audience threw me for a second, but then I rose to it and it felt completely natural, as if

I was born to act. We had never even rehearsed it on a proper stage.

During our two-week run at the theatre we were approached by a producer who toured plays around London's fringe venues, putting on performances in pubs and restaurants, and for the next six months we made several trips to London to perform the play. It was a real achievement for me. Not only was I using the play to put my own ghosts to rest, but I was proving to myself and the world that I could write and act. Most of all, I felt I was helping other people's knowledge and awareness of abuse.

Because I was very open about my abuse, I found other people coming to me to tell me their experiences. I listened and gave them advice about going for counselling. I didn't take my own advice, though: my GP had referred me to a psychiatrist a few years earlier, but I only saw him once. He suggested that my children should be taken into care for a few months so that I could go into an assessment centre for treatment to help clear my memories and nightmares. He asked me if I felt guilty because I enjoyed sex with my stepfather. I thought, This guy has no idea. I'm better off keeping myself strong.

As with all the men in my life, I made sure John knew about the abuse before we started our relationship. We were madly in love and it felt as though a positive new chapter was starting. My college work was also going well and the hard work soon paid off. I was thrilled to pass GCSEs in media and communications, sociology and English. It felt like a real vindication of the talent my teachers had spotted in me all those years ago, and which Mick Garvey had done his best to crush. I couldn't believe all the years I'd wasted feeling I was never going to achieve anything, and I felt great pride in myself that I had taken back one of the things he had snatched away from me.

John and I were very happy. He kept his own small flat

across the road from mine, and used it as an office for marking work and planning lectures, as well as studying for his degree. It was tiny: just room for a bed, desk, chair and cooker. His two younger children, Tony and Tricia, spent time with us, but his oldest, also called Sharon, who was in her late teens, didn't come. I think she thought it would be disloyal to her mother, which I fully understood.

Everything was going very well, but after a few months I heard some news that totally blighted my life. Recently my mother had been plagued by back and leg pain, but the doctors had kept fobbing her off with painkillers. Eventually her husband, John, who was a Mason, had taken her to the Royal Masonic Hospital, where she was given a CAT scan. The result was the worst it could be: she had lung cancer.

Why, God, why? I asked myself. Just when she is so happy. Can't our family ever enjoy some peace?

CHAPTER FIFTEEN

Mum had an operation to remove half of one of her lungs and it appeared to be a success. She made a reasonably good recovery and I dared to hope that all would turn out well. I spent as much time as I could in London with her, and John was wonderfully supportive. We were still very much in love, and whenever I hear Phil Collins's song 'Groovy Kind of Love' I think of those happy days. We danced together to it on our second date, when we were at Ricky Tomlinson's club.

At about this time I became a council tenant again, after the house in Parkfield Road was scheduled for demolition. We moved into a two-bedroom, second-floor flat in Linnet Lane.

Despite my hopes, we were soon to receive a tragic blow. Mum's cancer had spread to her brain, and she had to embark on a gruelling round of chemotherapy, radiotherapy, everything the doctors could throw at her. It was devastating for us all knowing she was so ill. I desperately wanted to do something, but I could only put my trust in the doctors and pray. She felt really rotten and by Christmas was very ill. She was determined to come up to spend New Year's Eve with us in Liverpool, but soon after she and John arrived she began to have terrible headaches. She couldn't stand noise or bright lights, was unable to hold her food down and spent most of the time lying in a darkened room.

But nothing would stop her coming out with us on New Year's Eve, and we all went to the Banjo Bar in the docks road.

It was a great night, with Gordon and Anne there too. Mum was so weak that she couldn't walk without help, and I had to take her to the toilets to be sick. She got snappy with me, telling me not to follow her everywhere. She was determined to be all right.

Ironically, she looked great. Just before Christmas John had taken her away for a holiday in the sun, and she was tanned and blonde. But although she looked good outwardly, inside she was ravaged with pain. The next day, New Year's Day, I called a doctor out and he gave her a painkilling injection and said we should get her home to the hospital where they were in charge of her treatment. He also recommended that John shouldn't take her on his own: she needed someone to look after her in the car. The tumour was now pressing on her brain and some of her actions were becoming irrational.

John happily looked after my boys while I made the journey with Mum and John, on one occasion forcibly having to stop her climbing out of the car door as we travelled down the motorway at high speed. Eventually she lay down on the back seat and I crouched in the footwell, holding her hand until she drifted off to sleep.

After a couple of days in hospital she was allowed home, and I went back to Liverpool. Her illness and her impending death were never discussed: it was like the abuse; everyone seemed to think it was better kept under wraps. At the same time that Mum was ill her best friend Eileen's husband Dave also had terminal cancer, and I like to think they were able to talk to each other and share their fears of dying.

After I had been home for about a week John rang to say she was back in hospital and it didn't look good. I arranged for David, who was ten at this time, and Gordon, who was eight, to stay with Donna while I went back to London. For the first week me, John, Phil and Tom slept at home and spent our days with her, but she started ringing at all times through the night.

'Sharon, I can't deal with this pain. Get me some tablets.'

When I told the hospital staff, they said she couldn't have any more painkillers or she would overdose.

'Let her overdose. It's better than what she's going through. I'll pay you – just give her what it needs to take the pain away.'

I even collected as many painkillers as I could find in the house and took them with me when I went to the hospital, but fortunately when I got there she was OK, as they had increased her medication.

She hated being so ill: 'Sharon, look at the state of me. My hair's come out.'

I told her not to worry, and I pampered her, washing her face and arms and legs, rubbing cream into her dry skin and tying a scarf round her head. I felt it was my turn to mother her and look after her, and I wanted to do everything I could to help, to be there for her.

When I was with her or my brothers, I tried to be cheerful and upbeat, but when I was on my own in bed at night, I sobbed silently into my pillow, careful not to wake anyone. I cried for her but I also cried for myself: it seemed so unfair that I was losing her just when our lives as mother and daughter were so perfect. We'd had a few wonderful years without Mick Garvey, and we had been as close as it is possible to be. I tortured myself with negative thoughts: Why do I always have to be punished? Is it because I shouldn't have been born, because she should have had that abortion and got rid of me?

I thought about that a lot, not blaming her but convincing myself that my whole life had been so bad because I should never have existed in the first place. Mum was in my head the whole time and my poor sleep patterns became worse. I couldn't eat and lost a lot of weight.

One day, when I was with her at the hospital, standing

behind her fixing her scarf, a little Malaysian cleaning lady said to her, 'Your daughter is very nice.'

My mum said the best words I ever heard her say: 'D'you know what, love, this is the best daughter any woman could ever wish to have. And one day she'll know how much I mean it, because I really love her.'

She had never been able to say it directly to me – it wasn't her way – but she said it to someone else for me to hear. To me, it was a very special moment and tears fell from my eyes as I busied myself with her scarf. I've treasured those few words, and they have come back to me whenever I have needed strength.

One day she asked me to get her some Hush Puppies shoes, like the nurses wore. I think she believed psychologically that if she had shoes, she would go somewhere, she would walk out of the hospital. They stayed new, in their box, by her bed, a forlorn symbol of hope.

Eventually she fell into a coma. I had been sitting by her bedside night and day for over a week, and I was able in that time to say everything I ever wanted to say to her. I was convinced she heard me telling her how much I loved her and how much she meant to me and to every one of her family. I told her that the abuse had not been her fault, and I absolved her of any guilt: 'You have only ever done your best for all of us. When the time comes, go to Nan and Granddad with open arms. I will always look after Tom and Phil.'

I didn't want to leave her side, didn't want to do more than doze next to her, in case she needed me. I was overwhelmed by my love for her, and the only way left that I could express it was to be with her night and day. Eventually I was so tired that one of the doctors said that if I didn't go for a sleep, he would inject me to make sure I got some rest.

I told Mum, 'I'm going for a sleep now. If you love me, wait for me to come back before you go. I'll never forgive you if you go while I'm not here. You've got to wait for me, and if you do, I'll know you love me.'

I hugged her and went to the room the hospital had given to us to sleep in. Other members of the family had arrived now, to sit with her, so I knew she wasn't alone, which was important to me. It was about 10 a.m., and I instantly fell into a deep sleep, fully clothed, on the bed. At dead on quarter to six in the evening I woke up suddenly, as if I had been hit by a bolt of lightning. I jumped out of bed, ran along the corridor and down two flights of stairs to the day room on the ward, where all the family, apart from Gordon, who was with Mum, had congregated.

Anne said to me, 'I'll get you a cup of tea before you go in, wake yourself up.'

'No, I need to go in now. I'll have a cup of tea when I know everything is OK.'

I walked into Mum's room just as Gordon, who was leaning over her, said to the nurse, 'Her fingernails have gone blue. Is that normal?'

I went to the other side of her and put my arm under her head and whispered, 'I'm here now, Mum.'

She took her last breath as I held her. I know she had waited for me, she didn't reject me. In death, and by the timing of her death, she told me that she loved me. It meant everything to me.

She was only forty-six when she died. The family came in and everyone was crying, even the nurses, who had become so fond of her. I couldn't cry. It was as if the pain was too deep for tears. I was emotionally numb, unable to take in what I had lost. I went home to Liverpool to break the news to David and Gordon, and they found it very difficult to take. She had been a good grandmother to them. John looked after them while I went back for the funeral. Again, I functioned on autopilot, doing and saying all the right things, but deep inside feeling frozen and cold.

Despite being with her when she died and attending the funeral, it was as if her death still hadn't hit me. It took a couple of weeks to sink in. At the time she died David had been taking the entrance examination for a boys' grammar school. Mum had always been confident that he would get in, so when we heard that he had been accepted, without thinking I ran to the callbox and dialled her number. John answered.

'Is Mum there?' I said.

'Sharon…'

As he spoke it hit me, and I felt so guilty adding to his grief. 'Oh, God, John, I'm so sorry. What have I done?' When I put the phone down, it felt as though a tap had been turned on inside my emotions. I stood in the callbox sobbing and sobbing. All my grief was finally released.

Mum, I asked, in utter despair, why did you leave me? Why does everyone who loves me leave me?

It was as if my life was a series of tests, and as soon as one was over, another was thrown at me. Luckily, John was really good news at this time, wonderfully supportive, and we were very close.

Thankfully, out of my next round of bad luck came something truly wonderful. I had a routine smear test, which showed I had cancerous cells in my womb. This was yet more devastating news, especially so soon after Mum's death from cancer, and I started on a course of laser treatment. I was told the condition would only be completely cured if I had a hysterectomy. This made me profoundly sad, as although the time had never been right, I had always thought at the back of my mind that I would have another baby one day and that this time it would be a girl. I consoled myself with the fact that I had two lovely, healthy sons, and that was more than many women had.

Accepting that I had no option, I booked myself in for a pre-op assessment. To my huge surprise and great delight, they discovered I was pregnant. It really felt to me as though Mum was giving me a present, making sure that something good came to me after so much bad. John was thrilled too.

I was warned that pregnancy hormones could speed up the growth of the cancer cells and I was offered an abortion. I wasn't prepared to even consider it; I really wanted this baby.

I knew that if Mum had anything to do with it, my baby was going to be the little girl I had always wanted. I was so sure that I began buying ballet shoes and girly clothes from the second month of my pregnancy.

The pregnancy went well, but my baby was born six weeks early in August 1992, by Caesarean section, which was necessary because the laser treatment for my cancerous cells had caused so much scar tissue. When I awoke, there was the baby girl I'd longed for, only five pounds but a real little fighter who guzzled down her food hungrily. David and Gordon adored her, and John was a doting dad. We chose the name Courtney for her. I'd heard it first on *EastEnders* and loved it.

After I'd fully recovered from the birth, I had the hysterectomy. It was sad accepting the end of my chances and choices to have more children, because I'd always wanted a large family, but I needed to look after my health for the sake of the three children I had. My baby needed a mother. On another level, though, I was glad. To me, the operation symbolised the removal of Mick Garvey from my body finally and completely. It was as if the surgeon's knife had cut him out of me, and anything he had left behind was now gone. I felt cleansed by it. Until then, it was as if he still owned a bit of me, and had left his mark. But now all I had were memories. Nothing physical remained as witness to his power over me.

Soon after Courtney's birth I noticed that John was becoming distracted and was spending longer and longer at his own flat. I became unsettled by his long absences and eventually I couldn't tolerate it: I was determined, after Mum died, to live life on my own terms, not put up with anything I didn't like. At my insistence, we broke up. I was miserable, because I really loved him, but I couldn't live with insecurity. He came regularly to see Courtney and the boys, and I encouraged him.

I was still reeling from the shock of the breakdown of the relationship when more bad news hit me. Uncle Gordon turned up on my doorstep and I could tell from his expression that something bad had happened. I was putting Courtney to bed and he insisted I sit down on the bed before he told me.

'Don't tell me someone's died?' I asked, my heart hammering in my chest.

Gordon nodded sadly.

Please, God, don't let it be Tom or Phil. I don't think I can take much more.

It was Mum's husband, John, the lovely, gentle soul who had brought so much happiness into her last years. He died, I am convinced, of a broken heart. Without Mum, he simply didn't have the will to live.

John looked after the children while I went to London with Gordon. It was an unpleasant time, as there were disputes between Mum's family and John's. He had welcomed Mum's family as his own, just as we had taken him to our hearts. In his death, we felt we were being excluded. The wake was held at Mum's house, and predictably it was a terrible occasion. I was very upset: John's memory deserved better.

I decided to move back to London and take over Mum's

maisonette on Ackroyd Drive, because it felt like the only thing I had left of her. I wanted to be physically near to her memory. I also had a very strong need to be close to my brothers. Phil was still very young, only twenty-two, and I felt we needed to be together with Tom. Our anchor, Mum, had gone, and with John dead, it felt that if I didn't take over the home, we would all be dispersed.

Although it had been the scene of some unhappy events in my life, in the ten years that Mum had lived on Ackroyd Drive with John, we had created many good memories. It had always been Mum's home; I only ever regarded Mick Garvey as a hanger-on, so it was never his place. And when Mum and John lived there, it had become somewhere I felt safe and loved. A house is just a house, a room is just a room – what matters is the human beings who live there. As far I was concerned, the place belonged to Mum and John.

I did still have flashbacks, but I knew by now that they could happen wherever I was living, even in places that had no connection to anything that had happened, like Inverness. I'd learned to expect them and live with them. They came from inside me, and I accepted I would always have them.

I went to see the council and they agreed to transfer the tenancy to me. Although it had already been transferred once – when Mum had died and it went to John – they were happy to bend the rules. It was a big decision for me: only a few days earlier the council in Liverpool had offered me a bigger flat, a lovely ground-floor one with three bedrooms.

The move was softened for the children because they had stayed so often at Mum's place in Ackroyd Drive that it was already like a second home to them. They settled into their schools – David went to the same secondary school that I had attended – and we began to put down new roots.

Soon after we moved in, the phone rang.

'Who's that?' a man's voice growled on the other end of the line.

I immediately recognised Mick's voice and for a split second I froze, the old fear stirring in the pit of my stomach. Then my anger surfaced. 'Sharon,' I answered calmly. Before he could say anything else, I said, 'Are you ever going to admit that you raped and abused me when I was a kid?'

There was a pause before he said, 'No I didn't.'

'Yes you did. Yes you did. Did you think it went away that easily?' My voice was rising as all my fury bubbled up.

'You're a liar. You're off your head, you are. I always said you were mental. This just proves it.' He slammed down the phone.

I was shaking and had to sit down for a minute or two and breathe deeply to calm myself. Then I very deliberately put him out of my head, repeating to myself, You're nothing to me now. I'm not afraid of you.

It would be a few more years before our paths would cross again – although, like I'm sure happens to all victims of abuse, there was never a day when what he had done to me wasn't present in my thoughts at some point.

CHAPTER SIXTEEN

We lived in Mum's old home for a few months before we were evicted by the council. Unfortunately, someone there found out that the rules had been bent when the tenancy was transferred to me, so they had no option but to ask me to move out. It was heartbreaking, not just for me and my three children, but also for Tom and Phil who, although they didn't live there, still visited every day and regarded it as their family home.

All I was offered as accommodation for me, David, Gordon and Courtney was a hostel for the homeless, and I certainly wasn't going to take my kids to a place like that. Liverpool Council couldn't help me either, because I was deemed to have made myself homeless when I quit my flat there after John had died.

So I went up to Liverpool for a few days, dragged myself round all the letting agencies and eventually found us a place in Alwyn Street, again in the Lark Lane area. It was a mess, but I'm never put off by the hard work of cleaning and decorating. My insomnia means that my family can go to bed and get up the next day to find I've transformed an entire room.

At first I was totally preoccupied with homemaking, but I was soon to discover great happiness in the shape of a beautiful hunk of a man. I first saw him as I was walking to the corner shop with Courtney in her buggy, and I was wearing my blue paint-spattered overalls, because I was still busy trying to lick the flat into shape.

Walking towards us was a friend of mine, Marty, and with him was this apparition: a tall, strong-looking man with gorgeous teeth and eyes, and long salt-and-pepper hair down to his shoulders. He was my dream man, and as I neared them, I honestly thought, I'm in love with you. You're the most gorgeous man I've ever seen.

Marty introduced us, and I wasn't put off even when I heard that the man's name was Mick. I didn't see him again until a few weeks later, when I was out for the evening with Donna and a couple of girlfriends, who were determined to cheer me up. In the bar we saw Marty, and he called us across to sit with his mates, and there was Mick again. He came and sat with me and chatted, and we discovered we had been in primary school together. He is four years younger than me, and I laughed when I remembered a little snotty-nosed kid I had once had to look after. It was incredible that he could have grown into this amazing-looking man.

He walked me home and we talked all night. Following my own rules, I told him everything about the abuse, and he, in turn, told me about his childhood. We connected on so many levels, and the hours flew by as we poured out our life stories. In the morning he left, borrowing my iron and promising to give it back soon.

When he didn't return the iron, my newfound love turned to anger, especially after I had to borrow my neighbour's iron to get the children's uniforms pressed for school. After a few days I went round to his address and banged on the door. He answered wearing nothing but boxer shorts. I could feel my stomach dropping with desire for him, but my anger prevailed and I walloped him in the chest.

'Who do you think you are, keeping my mother's iron?' I challenged him. 'Don't take the piss out of me. You're not who I thought you were.' It must have looked absurd, my five feet two inches to his six feet three, but I was furious, wagging my finger at him. 'Get me that iron now.'

Sheepishly, he did, and I stormed off as soon as he'd handed it over.

A couple of days later David said to me, 'Some fella keeps walking up and down our street.'

I looked out, and it was Mick, but he never plucked up the courage to come to the door, and I was too proud to go to him.

A few days later we met again when I persuaded Donna and the others to go to the same bar. I played it cool, but when I spotted him, it was all I could do to contain my excitement. We linked up again, and again he walked me home. Only this time he stayed.

It took me a few months to be able to call him 'Mick'. At first he was just 'babe', until I overcame my aversion to the name, but in those early months that was our only problem. We were madly, wildly in love. We couldn't get enough of each other. Our friends dubbed us John and Yoko, because whenever they called round we'd come to the door wrapped in a sheet. It was a deep, animal passion, but it was also a meeting of minds and hearts, a real friendship. Just as Donna is my female soulmate, Mick is my male soulmate.

But it was not happy ever after. We were both damaged by our past experiences and we brought a lot of baggage to the relationship. My whole life had been shaped by loss: almost everyone I loved and trusted had, eventually, left me, and deep inside I felt it was all my fault. A little child who is abused is brainwashed from an early age to feel worthless, and my love for Mick was corrupted by fear and jealousy. I was convinced that he, too, would leave me.

His fears were even bigger than mine, and after six months of pure bliss our relationship began to distort horribly. One night, when he was very drunk, Mick's terrors spilled out into vicious verbal abuse, followed by a savage beating. It was the first time in many years that my body had been battered. As I crawled out of bed the next day and inspected my bruises, the sensible voice in my head said, Walk away. Walk away now. You've come a long way to get over the violence of your childhood. Don't repeat it.

But there was a different drumbeat in my head: He's said sorry. He regrets it. That's more than Mick Garvey ever did. He's different. He's a good man. It's just the drink talking.

I could see an innate goodness in him, and I suppose, like my mother and so many other battered wives before me, I felt I could change him. It wasn't the last time he hit me, but the violence only happened when he was drunk, which was different from my stepfather, who was aggressive and domineering even when sober.

We struggled with our relationship for a full three years, and there were bad times. Even so, both of us believed that what we had between us was worth fighting for. There was no magic solution of course. We tried moving to an area where nobody knew us, in North Wales, but the pattern continued. It was a vicious circle familiar to many abusive relationships: Mick drank because he felt bad about the way he treated me. He drank for oblivion, but instead the drink made him repeat the behaviour he was trying to forget.

I think it helped that when he was sober, I could verbalise my fears. Sometimes he would arrive home and I would smell drink on him and he'd say, 'I only had a couple of cans in the van on the way home with the lads.'

I would reply, 'I know, but the smell of alcohol frightens me.'

I think we reached a turning point in Mick's drinking one Christmas when he brought a bottle of brandy home. I didn't want it in the house, as I was terrified of alcohol being around him. He had a go at me for being so puritanical. In anger and frustration that he couldn't see my point, I grabbed the bottle and smashed it over his head. It cut his head open, and there was blood streaming down his face. I calmly rang the police and told them to come and arrest me.

When two cops arrived, they faced me and Mick, both demanding to be arrested, vying to have the handcuffs put on.

Mick said, 'Don't nick her. I'm no good to her the way I am. It's all my fault. She needs to be here for the kids.'

But I held my hands out and said, 'I want to be arrested. I want to be out in a cell where I can sleep, eat three meals a day and not worry about anyone else. It's me you should arrest – I hit him with the bottle.'

We were both so earnest and desperate to be the one at fault that the policemen started laughing, and that started us off laughing too. They left without arresting either of us.

Another crisis was averted, but it made me give Mick an ultimatum: 'I'm moving back down South to be near my brothers, so that I feel safe. You can come, but you have to promise to do something about the drinking.'

I wanted another fresh start, and I also wanted to be near Tom and Phil again, because I felt they would protect me if I ever needed it. By this time David, having left school at sixteen, had moved down to stay with Tom, and I really missed him and wanted all my children together again. Gordon was also now about to leave school, so it was a good time to move.

We found flats in Essex, but despite his promises, it seemed as though Mick hadn't changed. He found work immediately – throughout our time together he has always worked hard – but there were still occasional lapses into drunkenness and violence, and I gave him a final choice: 'You can come with me to counselling or we can split up now and never see each other again.'

Mick really wanted to change, and we went together to the first two counselling sessions. Then something unexpected happened. The counsellor took me to one side and told me that I didn't need to come any more, as he would see Mick on his own. He said he didn't think I had any problems that needed his help. I was really surprised, because throughout the years since the abuse had started, I felt I had battled to keep myself sane and to appear normal, but inside I felt I was still damaged. The counsellor said, 'The last two sessions have shown me that you have worked through your own problems very successfully. You have confronted and dealt with all your own issues. I can help your partner, but you have helped yourself.'

I saw him again later, when I gave Mick a lift to his counselling session, and he asked me if I would like to train as a counsellor myself: 'You've done a marvellous job on yourself.'

It was the first time anyone had ever praised me for the way I had survived and coped, and I was shocked. I had learned my survival techniques through necessity, and I had never thought of them as anything special. But the counsellor sowed a seed in me: an idea that one day I would use my experiences to help others.

The counselling really helped Mick. He stopped drinking and since that point he has been the kindest, strongest, loveliest man, completely supportive of me, and focused only on his home, family and job. It took a little while to rebuild a good relationship with David and Gordon, who had witnessed the violence, but they always respected the fact that I loved Mick, and eventually they were able to see that my love was well founded. Now we all get on together brilliantly.

Looking back, I can see that Mick and I healed each other. We both had a lot of anger and frustration to get rid of, and we vented it on each other. It was very destructive for a time, but it meant we purged all the negative parts of our relationship. We were the best possible therapy for each other.

It is nine years now since Mick gave up drinking and he has proved to be everything and more than I could have wished for in a man. We belong together, we fit together perfectly, and I have, with Mick, found the happiness I never thought I deserved or could achieve.

While my love life was coming together successfully, there were important developments in another part of my life, my unfinished business with Mick Garvey. Although he had well and truly disappeared from my life, he hadn't disappeared from my mind. How could he? His actions had defined my life, made me who I was. I had a vague idea that one day I would get even with him.

Some day, somehow, we will meet again, I promised myself. And this time I will emerge the winner.

CHAPTER SEVENTEEN

I was too busy with my own life to work out what I would do to bring Mick Garvey to account. I was happy, my day-to-day routine was great, my family was all around me, and Mick was sober and loving. Then one night I had a vivid dream about Mick Garvey. I still had occasional nightmares, when my Mick would hold me and comfort me, but this dream was different. I saw his face clearly, but I wasn't frightened by it.

The following day was a bright, sunny September day in 2002. I can remember everything in sharp focus. Mick was at work, David, who was living at home again, was out, Gordon was in his room with his music on, playing computer games, and Courtney was playing with friends in her bedroom. The doorbell rang, and on the step was my brother Phil. I knew that over the years Mick Garvey had kept some loose contact with Phil, who was his son, but Phil had made sure he never mentioned it to me. Besides, it wasn't the sort of contact you had with a real father: there were no birthday cards or Christmas presents for Phil.

I was pleased to see Phil and immediately stepped aside to usher him in. As I did so, I realised that there was someone with him: John Garvey, Mick's younger brother. I hadn't seen John for many years, probably not since the time he had kidnapped Phil back from America. I recognised him immediately. I had never disliked him, despite associating him with his brother, and we had all been very grateful to him for the rescue of Phil, but it was still a huge surprise to find him on my doorstep.

We sat down with a cup of tea, and then Phil said he had to go and see someone. He left me alone with John. I had no idea what was going to happen next.

'I've got something to tell you,' he said seriously. 'And I know you are going to be upset.' He took a deep breath and continued, 'My brother, who abused you, also abused me when I was a kid. He raped me when I was eleven.'

My first response was anger. I thought, You knew he was a child abuser all those years he lived with Mum and us. Why didn't you do something?

But then I could see he had obviously been traumatised by what had happened to him, and I knew how easy it is for a domineering bully like Mick Garvey to ensure that people stay silent. My anger turned to pity, and I felt tears welling in my eyes at the thought of all the years he must have suffered in silence. I felt very sorry for him, and also a deep sense of relief: what he had told me was proof that Mick Garvey really was a monster, and that it wasn't just me who knew it.

'I know you've been saying my brother abused you. I believe you,' he said.

Those three words, 'I believe you', meant a great deal to me. Although by this time my family and friends knew and believed, I was now hearing it from someone who was not close to me, and who had every reason to try to suppress what he knew about his brother.

He explained how he was scared, embarrassed, ashamed to do anything about it. He was very upset. I thought of all the years he had shadowed his brother, in awe of him, and I realised for the first time that he must also have been truly terrified of him, which made his act of rescuing Phil even more courageous.

I don't know to this day why he decided to come to see me when he did. Suddenly, my normal afternoon had gone and I was back in a maelstrom of emotions about my own abuse. I saw very clearly that day that however much I tried to bury the abuse, it was never far beneath the surface.

'What are you going to do?' I asked John.

'Do you know what? I'm going to the police,' he said, as if seeing me had hardened his resolve. 'He's living in America now, so I don't suppose anything can be done. But I'm going to tell them about him.'

'I promise you that if you go, so will I,' I replied determinedly. It wasn't something I had considered until that moment, but I saw instantly that this was the push I had been needing to make me do something.

John left with the assurance that he would go through with it. I felt comfortable, and I even slept peacefully for the next two nights. I had no worries about my abuse being made public: I had told my children since they were old enough to understand, starting when they were very young by drilling into them that they could tell me anything, that I would always believe them. 'Mum got very badly hurt when she was a little girl,' I told them, 'because she didn't think anyone would believe her. I need you to know that you can tell me anything, and mums have magic eyes and know when children are telling the truth.'

I made sure that by the time they were seven or eight they understood the need not to let anyone do anything to them against their will. I believe that most paedophiles choose children between the ages of about seven and ten, so I felt it was crucial to arm them. I didn't want to scare them away from all adults, but I explained in a non-frightening way that if ever they got the feeling that someone was too close, invading their space, they should scream, spit, kick, punch, scratch, anything to make themselves heard and get them out of the situation. As they got older, I gave them more general information about my abuse, and I told them how having them had helped me survive. Every single day I told them how much I loved them, and they knew I would do anything to protect them.

So there was no worry that hearing about my abuse would be a shock to them, and I had been honest with the rest of my family. Mick knew everything. Now all I had to do was to wait for John to tell me that he had gone to the police and I would follow suit.

But on the third night I had a premonition in my sleep. It was not a dream, it was different. I saw a small cell, with a window high up, and a man with his back to me sitting on a hard chair. Beside him stood four prison guards, all in uniform, and all with the same face, like clones. I was standing in the doorway to the cell when suddenly the man turned and looked at me. It was my stepfather. I knew they were waiting to take him somewhere. I also knew that the place where he was imprisoned was not in this country, but was in France, Spain or Italy.

When I woke up, I felt very strong, and as if I was on a cloud floating above all my problems. I knew something special had happened. I said to Mick, 'I'm going to the police station.'

'What for?' Mick asked, startled.

'I know where Mick Garvey is. He's not in America. And he's in prison.'

'Sharon, please don't tell the police that you dreamed where he is. They'll think you're a nut.'

'I don't care. I'm not waiting for John any longer. I am doing it today,' I replied firmly.

I rang the local police station before my resolve could waver, and said the words that had been on my lips my whole life. 'I want to report a case of child abuse.'

CHAPTER EIGHTEEN

I explained to the policeman who took my call that I was forty-two years old, and that I had been abused throughout my childhood. What's more, my abuser was now in a foreign jail.

'How do you know?'

'I saw him there, in a dream.'

The man on the other end of the line coughed, to cover up a snort of laughter. It was like my Mick said: he thought I was mad. But I told him enough about my childhood for him to take at least some of my story seriously, and he made an appointment for me to see a police officer at the child abuse centre in Brentwood, a house specially designed in a relaxing and informal way so that victims of abuse can talk freely.

It may sound odd, but I didn't really care whether the police believed me or not. The last time I had spoken to someone official about the abuse, I hadn't been believed, and a large part of me didn't expect to be believed this time. But I wanted to put my story on the record. Even if they believed me, I was sure it was all too long ago for anything to happen. I wasn't expecting any kind of justice. I simply felt a strong need to take the first steps against Mick Garvey, not to let him get away with it any longer. I knew it would be painful, but my flashbacks were painful anyway. If John Garvey was strong enough, so was I.

It was at the abuse centre I met Lorna Henderson, a child protection officer with Essex Police. She was wonderful, the right person in the right job. I felt completely at ease with her, and she let me pour out my whole story. She was very professional, asking a few questions but in general just being happy to let me talk. It took four days of interviews to get down a sixteen-page statement covering my life from the age of four to seventeen. Every day after dropping Courtney at school I drove to Brentwood and carried on where I had left off.

It felt good to tell someone everything. I had never given all the details to anyone before. I was astonished how much I could remember: I had filed all the memories away in sealed compartments in my head, and when I opened them, it all came out. It was as if I had put my pain away very carefully, under different headings, as another survival technique. Now I felt a compulsion to empty it all out, into one big bag, and then hand it to someone else to deal with.

Lorna warned me not to get my hopes up, as it is difficult to get a conviction in a case of historic abuse. I told her about my dream of my stepfather languishing in a foreign jail, and she treated it seriously and said once the investigation was complete Interpol would be alerted.

I heard that John Garvey's allegations against his brother were not going to be proceeded with. I was shaken by this news, as I felt together we had a better chance and now I was alone. Why do I have to do everything on my own? I asked myself. Looking back, though, I'm glad that nobody else was involved.

The police set about getting more evidence. Because the abuse happened in Liverpool initially, and had never taken place in Essex, the case was transferred to Merseyside Police, where Detective Sergeant Peter Cain took over as the investigating officer. He is a good man, carved out of the same wood as Lorna Henderson. They both kept it real for me, letting me know that the chances of it going to court were slim, but at the same time dedicating a lot of time and effort to try to get justice for me.

The police took statements from my real dad, my brother Tom, Uncle Gordon and Donna. They all corroborated what I'd said. My dad was completely frank and honest, and admitted he was scared of Mick Garvey and really regretted not going to the police when I first told him. Donna was able to say that she had heard about my abuse since we were little children together. Uncle Gordon could confirm that I had been talking about it for a few years. And Tom remembered the occasion when he had banged on the wall and yelled at Mick to leave me alone. The police even tried to trace the Salvation Army colonel to whom I had told everything, but he had died.

At last, with the final statement in, Interpol was alerted. Four days later DS Cain rang me: they had tracked Mick Garvey down to Madrid, where he was just coming to the end of a four-and-a-half-year sentence for cannabis smuggling. Incredibly, my premonition had been right, and my timing had also been inspired: if I had waited any longer it may have been too late to trace him to the jail, as he was released three weeks later.

Building the case against him took time, and he couldn't be arrested straight away, so he walked out of jail a free man. This devastated me. I felt we had come so near but were still so far. It was vital he didn't have a clue that the British police were after him, or he could have disappeared to a country that was beyond their extradition reach. My biggest fear was that he would be tipped off, and for that reason I told only three people the full situation: my Mick, Donna and Uncle Gordon. The Spanish police kept him under very discreet observation, and the long waiting game began. It was an anxious time for everyone involved in the case, but somehow, deep inside me, I knew it was going to be OK.

However, I was suffering for having opened all the boxes in my head. The nightmares came crashing back, and I didn't let myself sleep in order to avoid them. It was like being a child again, staying awake listening for the creak of a floorboard or the turn of a door handle. When I did sleep, I would cry and scream, and my Mick had to hold me tight to stop me lashing out, all the time whispering to me, 'You're safe, Sharon, you're with me. He can't get you.'

This went on for nearly a year before, finally, the paperwork to arrest Mick Garvey was complete. He so nearly escaped. He was actually arrested at Madrid Airport, waiting to board a plane to South America with the latest woman in his life and their five-year-old daughter – apparently the police had received a tip-off that he was leaving. When I heard about the little girl, a shiver ran down my spine. If he hadn't been arrested when he was, who can say what might have happened to her? I was overjoyed he had been caught in time. By saving her from him, it was almost as if I was saving my five-year-old self. I was redeeming myself by rescuing her.

On the night I heard he was arrested, I received a call from DS Cain: 'Just to let you know that Mick Garvey has been arrested at Madrid Airport. He's in custody in Spain, and we're working on getting him extradited.'

'Wow, I can't believe it.' A surge of relief washed over me. I caught my breath before continuing, 'That's just great.'

When I put the phone down, I cried and cried. Mick was worried, until I explained I was crying with sheer pleasure – it was a release of the tension of knowing that he was still out there. It made me happy to think that he had been taken back to the same jail where he had served his sentence for smuggling: to me, that was the jail that appeared in my dream. It was satisfying to think he wasn't there this time as a drug trafficker, a big criminal; now he was there as a paedophile, the lowest of the low, something that crawled out from under a stone. I don't know how Spanish prisons operate, but I can't imagine the other prisoners are any kinder to sex offenders who prey on children than they are here.

I also relished the fact that his arrest must have come as a complete shock to him, and when he was told he was being arrested for what he had done to me, it must have made him furious. He was my worst nightmare as a child, but now I was back, and about to become his worst nightmare. He took the beginning of my life; I was going to take the end of his.

I also had other, less positive, feelings, though. I was afraid of what was in store – the prospect of reliving it all in court – and I knew I was putting a lot of strain on my kids, Mick, my brothers, Uncle Gordon, my real dad, Donna and everyone who cared about me. I felt guilty for them, and there was a large part of me that said, Why didn't you let it go, forget about him and get on with our life?

The police were very good about keeping me in touch, and so, too, was Lionel Copes, the solicitor for the Crown Prosecution Service who handled the case. Lionel proved to be a diamond, a real rock throughout the coming months. When, after about three months, the extradition was cleared, DS Cain let me know that he would be flown back to Britain and taken to Walton Jail. I was pleased to hear he was in Walton, the prison where I had visited him as a child, and which I knew he hated. It felt as though everything had come full circle.

A couple of months later the police told me that he was going to appear in court, by a video link from the jail, for a plea hearing, at which he would plead guilty or not guilty. I decided to go to the hearing. I didn't have to go: no evidence would be heard; it was simply a matter of him registering his plea and the judge remanding him in custody.

My Mick said, 'Why put yourself through this? You won't even really see him on the video link.'

But I felt strongly that I wanted to see his face before I had to confront him in court. I needed to see what he looked like. Was he still the monster of my memory? I went to Liverpool by train and stayed with Donna. She came to Liverpool Crown Court with me. It is a new building, very different from the magistrates court where I had appeared all those years ago. There is a staircase made from reinforced glass, which gives it a futuristic look. There are more than sixty courtrooms, so it is an overwhelming size, and always busy, with banks of lifts, large, carpeted public areas and a big canteen.

After passing through the security checks at the door, I explained to one of the ushers why I was there.

She said, 'Look, sweetheart, you're going to put yourself through a lot of pain. You don't have to be here.'

'I know I don't have to be here, but I *need* to be here,' I replied firmly.

She told me that Mick Garvey's barrister was in one of the side rooms, talking to my stepfather on the video link, and that she had to take some papers in. She explained that if I was standing behind her when she opened the door, I would be able to see him. It was kind of her. I think she could see that this was something that would help me.

I stood exactly where she told me, and as the door swung open, I could see a big screen, with his face filling it. It was him all right, the same monster. He looked older, his hair was thinner on top, but I could tell he was still a big man.

I felt tears hit my eyes and I willed myself not to cry. I turned to face Donna and almost fainted into her arms. She walked me across to a seat, where I sobbed and sobbed. I kept repeating, 'He hasn't changed. He's still there, still the monster.' I felt like a child again, very vulnerable.

In a way, the fact that he was so instantly recognisable made me more determined. But at that moment it hit me hard. I was very glad I had insisted on seeing him, because I didn't want to collapse and cry when I faced him in court. I thought, If I can get my weakness out of the way now, it will be the strong Sharon who stands in the witness box.

Going to the remand hearing was a wise decision. I'd had the shock, and I knew what I had to face. I'd confronted the demon, looked into his face without him knowing I was there, and this helped me banish all the power he had once held over me. My initial feelings of fear were soon replaced by strength.

After I'd recovered, we went into the public gallery of the court, heard him plead not guilty in that same loud, gruff voice and saw him again on the video link. This time Donna could see him too, and she shivered involuntarily. It was over very quickly. He didn't apply for bail – his solicitor must have told him he wouldn't get it.

Then I was in another waiting game. It was more than six months later that the court case began, almost two years since I had made my original statement to the police. I spent the time preparing. I went to the library and started reading legal textbooks. It was dry and boring mostly, but I forced myself to do it: I wanted to go to court armed with a reasonable amount of knowledge about how the legal system works.

I'd had flashbacks to the abuse all my life, but now, as I went over it all in my mind, they came more often and were terrifying. I taught myself to deal with them: Breathe deeply, stay calm. It will pass. It's just a memory, and it can't hurt you now.

When the date for the trial finally arrived, the Crown Prosecution Service arranged for me and Tom to have rooms at the

Moat House Hotel in Liverpool, as we had to travel up from London. Mick couldn't come with me, as he had to work, and we had to keep family life as normal as possible for Courtney, who was only twelve. To keep me company, Donna moved into my double room at the hotel with me, bringing her younger daughter, Mackenzie, who was then five years old. Having the little one there was a wonderful distraction, something else to think about other than the case.

As soon as I arrived at court, the Victim Support people took me, on my own, to a private room. They gave me a cup of coffee, but I was kept separate from my family and the other witnesses. I couldn't understand it: Why do I have to sit here on my own? I asked myself, bewildered. I'm not the one on trial.

After about ten minutes I decided that I would much rather be in the public area with my Tom and Donna, so I went and joined them. To my surprise, my brother Phil also turned up at court. I felt a huge rush of emotion when he walked in, and was so pleased he was there. I gave him a hug, and we talked about other things, not what was about to happen. He had known for years what I accused his dad of, but it was still his father in the dock, being tried for abusing his sister. I was very moved by his situation; he was riddled with guilt, pain, shock, horror. Also, he had been treated differently by Mick Garvey: whereas Tom and I had no good memories and hated the man who had blighted our child-hoods, for Phil it was different.

There was so much I wanted to say to him, but the main message was – and still is – that to Tom and me he is a full brother, not a half-brother, and he is nothing to do with that man. He is one of us, and we couldn't possibly love him more than we do. From the day he was born we have never linked him with his biological father. None of these important feelings were spoken that day at court, but I think Phil knew. It must have been as big an ordeal for him as it was for me. I hope my hug said the words for me.

Phil pointed out Mick Garvey's girlfriend. She didn't look his type: she was very quiet, subdued and respectable. But then, did he ever have a type? He could go from women to children, from boys to girls. The woman looked uncomfortable and out of place, and I felt sorry for her. She was his victim in the same way that Mum had been, and I'm sure it had all come as a shock to her too.

For the first two days the jurors were sworn in and the opening statements were made to the court by the Crown Prosecution barrister, David Owen, and the defence barrister. No witness is allowed in court before they are called to give evidence, so we had to hang around outside the courtroom. It seemed strange, and very unnerving, to wait outside once it had all begun. My stomach was tied in a knot and I couldn't eat.

I was the first witness, and when I walked up to the box, my presence made maximum impact on one person in the courtroom: the defendant. I didn't look at him, but I could feel his eyes on me and heard him let out an audible gasp. This was the reaction I had aimed for: I strongly resemble my mother, and for the trial I had made myself look as much like her as possible. I'd put the sides of my hair up into a little ponytail on top of my head, but with some tendrils coming down at the back, and a fringe, just like she had. I had drenched myself in her much-loved perfume, Estée Lauder Youth Dew, and I had bought a pale blue trouser suit, because that was her favourite colour and she felt she looked her best in it.

When I'd looked in the mirror before leaving the hotel, even I had done a double take. It was my mum looking back at me. The transformation was even better than I could have imagined, and I know it shocked Mick Garvey. I had wanted her there in the courtroom with me, haunting him. I wanted him to know that I was mother and daughter in one, that he didn't just have me in the witness box giving evidence against him, she was there too. I wore the same outfit every day, hurriedly washing it at the hotel in the evenings.

When I stood in the witness box, I received several good omens. First of all, the judge looked remarkably like my mum, apart, of course, from her iron-grey legal wig. Then I heard her name: Judge Elizabeth Steel. It seemed an appropriately strong-sounding name. And when I heard the name of Mick Garvey's barrister, Julian Nutter, I was even more happy: 'Nutter' was what Donna and I had nicknamed Mick Garvey when we were children.

It's me and Judge Steel against the paedo and the Nutter, I reflected wryly. No contest. How can we lose?

As I stood there in the witness box, I really felt that Mum and Nan were up in Heaven helping me. However terrible it was going to be for me, they had let me know that they were there, rooting for me.

Mr Owen, my barrister, took me through the story of my childhood with Mick Garvey, which I had outlined in my long statement to the police. Although standing up in court was an ordeal for me, and I was very nervous, he was respectful and considerate in his questioning. I kept my gaze averted from Mick Garvey, but I could feel his eyes boring into me.

Next, Mick Garvey's barrister, Mr Nutter, got up to cross-examine me. I realise that to him picking apart facts is a job, nothing more than another day at the office, but to me it was devastating. He tried to trip me up about tiny details of my evidence, and the main thrust of his questioning was to establish that I was a liar and a fantasist. In order to defend Mick Garvey, he had to discredit me, and he certainly did his best.

He said that I was making up the stories of abuse by my stepfather to avenge him for the way he had treated my mother. If this was revenge, I asked rhetorically, why did I leave it so long? I said I was not there for revenge but for justice.

At one point he said, 'You have got all your answers prepared, haven't you?'

I said firmly, 'No, you can't prepare the truth. I have just come here to tell the truth and there is no preparing of it. I am not lying.'

Thinking he had cornered me, he replied, 'You see, that is precisely the point, isn't it? We can't prepare the truth but you have got prepared answers to all the questions I have been putting to you, haven't you?'

I came back with, 'No, it is because I am answering you straight away directly with what I know to be true, and I am going to carry on doing exactly what I am doing now and answering you honestly with the truth.'

He went through the evidence in detail, trying to suggest that I only mentioned the Salvation Army man, Colonel Pratt, because I knew he was dead and couldn't contradict me. In fact, the defence had apparently been convinced I had invented Colonel Pratt, that he didn't exist, but they had then traced his brother, who had confirmed that he had worked at the Salvation Army building near Chrisp Street Market at the time I was there, but had died several years ago.

So when Mr Nutter said that I had used the colonel's name only because I was confident he couldn't contradict me, I replied simply, 'I see it the other way. I see that there was a man from over twenty years ago that I got help from that did exist. I can't prove what I said to him, but I remembered his name and I will never forget him for the help that he gave me.'

Mr Nutter was very concerned with small details, trying to trip me up. Was there a rug in the room at Knapp Road where

Mick Garvey raped me on the floor, or was it bare floor-boards? He argued with me about whether or not my stepfather contributed £2,000 to my wedding. I almost laughed out loud at the suggestion. 'He never had two thousand pounds,' I responded emphatically. 'The minute he gets any money, he blows it on wine, women and song. I am sorry, but that is a lie.'

I couldn't understand it: even if Mick Garvey had paid for my wedding (which he didn't), it wouldn't have meant that he hadn't abused me for thirteen years of my childhood. The whole object of the questioning was to establish that I was an unreliable witness. He was picking at me constantly, but I was determined not to let him wear me down. The clever thing about lawyers is that they ask you the same question in ten different ways, hoping to get you to contradict yourself. If you are telling the truth, though, they can't catch you out because you will always give the same answer. I am the sort of person who rises to a challenge, and I refused to let Mr Nutter fluster or confuse me.

He tried to imply that I was making myself out to be a victim because I was fascinated by other people's suffering. 'You are playing the role of a victim, aren't you?' he said.

'No, I am not a victim any more,' I replied definitely. 'I was, many years ago, but now I am a survivor, just like my mum was and just like anybody else that has been in this position and has come out the other side. I am a survivor.'

At one point Mr Nutter tried to suggest I was in court for financial gain, for compensation. Fortunately, through my legal research I knew that anyone abused within the home before 1976 doesn't qualify for compensation, so that demolished his attempt to make money my motivation.

He seemed preoccupied with finding my motivation. Sometimes he said things with which I could wholeheartedly agree. 'You have a burning resentment against Mr Garvey, do you not, because you see him as having destroyed your family life?'

'Yeah, I do,' I said nodding in agreement. 'I do see him as destroying not just my family life but my family. My mum was beaten on a regular basis. I was beaten and raped. My mother was put through the mill. My brothers were terrified...We have all suffered because this man was in our house. I don't hate him, because I wouldn't give him that much thought. I don't resent him; I wouldn't give him that much joy. I have no feeling towards him except for me to sort myself out. And also to let him know that he can't, for forty years, get away with this sort of thing. I am not letting him think that he can get away with one more day, because I am here just to say what I have to say.'

Judge Steel was amazing, allowing me to address the jury like this. Although it was draining being on the stand, and facing this barrage of questioning, adrenaline kicked in and carried me through. It wasn't until later that I would appreciate just how exhausting the cross-examination had been.

Whenever the courtroom was emptying and the judge had gone out, Mick Garvey would make death signals to me, drawing his hand across his throat, pointing his fingers in the shape of a gun at me. Others must have seen him, but nobody stopped him. I didn't allow it to get to me.

One of the hardest things about going through the details of my life in court was that it triggered a series of terrible memories, which I struggled to suppress. At one point, when Mick Garvey's barrister was going over and over the details of the furniture in the bedroom in Knapp Road, I felt exhausted and wanted to cry. At that moment I had a flashback to being four years old and Mick Garvey holding my arm up my back and kicking me repeatedly. Bang, bang – 'Don't you cry or I'll hit you more' – bang, bang. Up in the witness box, I started to shake and I felt as though I would collapse. I looked so ill the judge ordered a five-minute break.

Back on the stand, I felt another flashback to the same incident rising inside me, but I summoned the same resolve I had as a small girl when I would will myself not to let him see me cry. I told myself, He's kicking you. Stand up and smile. Stand up and smile.

It worked. In my head, I changed the image: instead of my stepfather scowling at me in fury as he kicked my small body, he was standing there shrugging his big shoulders, with his arms akimbo, as if to say, 'What are you doing?' I was able to carry on giving evidence coolly, and I was even able to look at him. I had defeated the memory.

I was on the witness stand for two days, a harrowing experience. After my evidence was over, I sat in the public gallery to watch the other witnesses give their evidence, but I couldn't stay there long: it was too difficult for me to see the pain of my friends and family. I felt I had put them all through this. I came into the courtroom halfway through my real dad's evidence, and when I heard how guilty he felt about not getting help for me, I was so, so sorry for him.

After six days the jury went out to consider their verdicts on the fourteen charges of rape and indecent assault, and we all waited, spending hours in the canteen, or just sitting in the public areas. We didn't dare leave the court building in case we missed the jury's return. After the first day of their deliberations I went back to the hotel for the night, confused, terrified and feeling that my life was hanging in the balance. If the jury found him not guilty, I felt it would be the latest in a long line of rejections in my life, and I would have to accept that the truth would never be recognised.

At last, the next day, the usher told us the jury was ready to deliver their verdicts. I felt as nervous as I had before the whole trial began; there were butterflies in my stomach and I had a vague feeling of wanting to be sick. I went into court with my family and sat with Donna and Uncle Gordon on either side, each holding one of my hands tight. The foreman of the jury stood up and delivered their verdicts: they found Mick Garvey guilty of the first rape of me, in the Harvey Hotel, but on all the other charges the jury were divided and couldn't reach a verdict.

My heart sank. To me, it seemed ridiculous. If they agreed that he had raped me once, how could they not see that he had raped me repeatedly? I felt angry and disappointed. We were all mystified as to how they had failed to reach verdicts, and very upset.

Mr Owen, however, was jubilant and, outside the courtroom, congratulated me. 'You've done a great job. He'll get eight years. Well done. We can go for a retrial if you want, but you don't want to put yourself through the stress. Let's call it a day.'

I didn't have to pause to think about it. I said firmly, 'I suffered nearly thirteen years of sexual abuse and yet he's only guilty of one rape. It's not right. I want a retrial. I am not walking away. I'll carry on fighting. If he gets eight years, he'll be out in four. Is that all he gets for destroying my life?'

The lawyer looked surprised. 'You've been so strong. A retrial would mean another long wait, a lot more stress.' He put his arm round me. 'Are you strong enough to do it all again?'

'Yes, I am.'

He nodded, convinced. 'You are one of the best witnesses I've had for many years. Let's go for it.'

I would have loved to have seen Mick Garvey's expression when he heard the news that I wasn't giving up.

CHAPTER NINETEEN

The second trial date was set for November, another four months away. Mick and all my family and friends were worried about me: they felt I should have been happy to have put him away for a few years on one rape. I felt guilty because I knew the other witnesses would have to go through it all again. The wait for the second trial was even more stressful than the first. I was permanently sick; I lost weight; I was angry and confused. How long do I have to live in this hell? When will it be over? Do I really deserve this?

I was told that the case might be heard before a different judge, and that I may not even have the same Crown Prosecution Service barrister, Mr Owen. This really stressed me out: Judge Steel, who looked like my mum, was a lucky talisman, and Mr Owen was so good it was hard to imagine having anyone else. Luckily for me, though, Mr Owen was able to represent our case for a second time, which was a great relief. When I finally got to the court, my first question to him was, 'Who's our judge?' When he said it was Judge Steel again, I was thrilled. He explained that she liked to see cases all the way through.

Before the case began, Mr Owen had asked me if there was anything I could add to the evidence I had given at the first trial, anything that would help prove the abuse happened. When he asked, I had a flashback to the time when I was eight years old and Mick Garvey was forcing me to have oral sex with

him. I saw again the sign of the cross, the symbol that I believed
Jesus sent to me to show that he was taking care of me.

'I'm not sure,' I had told Mr Owen cautiously. 'I'll tell you
something, but I want you to understand that I don't know
whether it is real or not. If I dreamed it and you reveal it in
court, it may make me seem like a liar...'

'Stop – go back to the beginning and tell me what it is,' he
said, keen to use any new evidence to our advantage.

So I explained to him that I opened my eyes just once
during oral sex, because I wanted to see what it was that was
killing me. 'I didn't know what he was putting in my throat,
what was stopping me breathing,' I explained, struggling for
words to describe the pain Mick Garvey had put me through.
'It makes no sense, but I just wanted to look before I died.
When I looked at his penis, I saw the sign of the cross, then I
conked out, and when I came round, I thought for a moment
or two that I had died.'

I had carried the image of the cross with me all my life, but
I had never mentioned it to anyone, not even Donna. Now,
after disclosing it to Mr Owen, I added, 'I don't think he really
has a cross on his penis. I believe it was a sign that I would
survive, and I did.'

But Mr Owen felt sure I had genuinely seen something,
and he wanted to present it as evidence in court. I was very
reluctant, afraid that the jury would think that if I was wrong
about this, then I must be lying about everything. Reluctantly I agreed and it was included in our case against Mick
Garvey.

I thought I would be less nervous for the second trial,
having gone through it once before, but I was still very on
edge. I knew that everything hung on me: the other witnesses
were there to back me up, but the whole case depended on the
jurors believing me. The fact that the first jury had only

partially believed me had thrown me a bit, but it had also made me even more determined not to let Mick Garvey's defence derail me. At least now I had more idea of what to expect. I told myself, over and over, that the truth would be heard. Mr Nutter can ask me the same question thirty different ways, but if I stick to the truth, the answer will always be the same, I resolved.

At the door of the court, I took a deep breath and switched into 'Bette Davis mode': as a little child, I'd seen those old black-and-white movies of the Hollywood star playing strong women and that was now my role model. I made sure my body language was strong, with my back straight and my head held high.

When I actually got into the witness box, the adrenaline once again kicked in. I was about to face another long verbal battle with Mr Nutter.

While I was in the witness box, I focused on the face of one juror, a middle-aged woman in the centre of the second row. For some reason, I felt that if she believed me, everybody would. I felt very sorry for some of the younger jurors: having to hear the details of the abuse I suffered must have been traumatic for them.

On the evening of my first day on the witness stand, something happened that was far more important to me than a victory over Mick Garvey. I'd returned to the hotel feeling drained, having not eaten all day. The phone rang at about 6.30 p.m., and it was my friend Kath, who was staying at my house to look after Courtney while Mick was at work. She was crying, struggling to get the words out. 'Courtney's run away,' she gasped.

I couldn't believe what I was hearing – it was so unexpected and out of character. Courtney was only twelve, and we were very close. But Kath continued, 'The woman next door has burned to death and Courtney couldn't save her. She's so upset she's run off.'

The woman who lived in the next flat to ours was an alcoholic and a drug user, and lived alone with her dog. Kath explained that she and Courtney had heard fire alarms going off, and when they had gone out on to the shared landing, it was full of smoke. They banged on the door of the woman's flat and she opened it in a drunken stupor, and refused to come out. Courtney grabbed her arm but she fought her off and went back inside, banging the door shut. After that, all Kath and Courtney heard were the howling of the dog and the screams as they perished in the fire. They couldn't get in or do anything to save her.

Trying to cope with what she had just witnessed, Courtney had then run out of the block, and apparently she had just kept on running, riven with guilt at not having been able to drag the woman out. I was distraught. I felt I had to choose between my daughter and my abuser, and for me there was no contest: I was going to get back home as fast as I could.

The case wouldn't be able to go ahead without me, because I had only just begun giving evidence, but I didn't care: I needed to find Courtney. This is when my baby needs me most, I thought. I have to be there for her.

I was hurriedly throwing my clothes into my bag when the phone rang again. It was Mick. He was home from work, and the police had found Courtney and brought her back. She was very upset, and when I spoke to her, she kept saying, 'I had hold of her, Mum. I had hold of her. I could have pulled her out but she pushed me off.'

I talked her through it, telling her how good and brave she had been, and how most people wouldn't have even tried to save the woman. I told her that the same thing would have happened to me if I'd been there, I wouldn't have been strong enough, and I explained that what she was feeling was natural after such a traumatic event.

'You'll never forget it, but you have to accept that you had no control over it,' I said softly, 'and you can't change things you have no control over.'

In spite of my calming words, inside I was bubbling with anger at the woman who had killed herself. Stupid, stupid woman, I cursed. She risked the lives of everyone in the block, and she hurt my Courtney.

After I'd calmed down Courtney, Mick spoke to me again. He told me I had to stay in Liverpool and see the trial through. I was completely torn. I had come so far with the case, but I knew that for me my present – my life with Mick and my children – far outweighed my past in importance. Donna, who was again staying with me at the hotel, eventually persuaded me to stay, and help me to unpack.

Again it was great having Mackenzie there in the evenings. I couldn't face going into the restaurant for a meal – I felt unclean and I thought everyone would look at me and see it – so we had room service in our bedroom, and I took Mackenzie swimming in the hotel pool. I missed Courtney badly, and Mackenzie was a good distraction.

It was hard to concentrate the next day, but once I was in the courtroom, my brain switched back into gear. As agreed, Mr Owen asked me about the cross on Mick Garvey's penis, and I told the jury, 'I really don't know if this is my imagination or if it was the truth, but as his penis was approaching me, I saw a cross. To me, that signifies God…It was a blue cross with dots around it, but it was on the end of his penis. And even today as an adult I can't say it was definitely there, but if not, it was like God trying to save me and saying, "It's all right, it's nearly over. Just look at the cross and think about Jesus and you're going to be OK."

'I don't know if he's got a tattoo there or if he hasn't, but I know that as a child that saved me, made me think of other things: God, Jesus and my nan.'

When the cross-examination began, it was another long battle with Mr Nutter, who on several occasions called me a liar and tried to trip me into admitting I was lying. He asked me in detail about the cross on my stepfather's penis: 'There was no cross on the end of his penis, was there?'

I replied, 'I wouldn't know, because as I've said, I'm not a hundred per cent sure if it's my memory or if it really happened.'

He then asked if I'd been told by someone else about the tattoo on Mick Garvey's penis. For the first time I was given confirmation that, whatever it was of, there was a tattoo there. He questioned me about it relentlessly, and I stuck to my guns.

'I saw a cross and that's my interpretation of it as a child. So thank you for letting me know he has one...I always believed he didn't have a tattoo. I was sure it was my imagination, that God was looking after me because I had to have something...

'If somebody had told me that he had a tattoo on his penis, they would also have told me what it was, and if I was lying, I would have said exactly what he had on his penis. I have discussed none of this with my family, his family, my friends.'

I was in the witness box for three harrowing days. On a couple of occasions I became very distressed, and Judge Steel was once again extremely sympathetic and let me have a break. One occasion was when we were going over my suicide bid with the pills, and another was when Mr Nutter was hammering me about when I had told my family and friends about the abuse. He was constantly trying to trip me up by comparing the exact words I had used at the first trial with what I said now. I felt as if I was the one on trial, not Mick

Garvey, but I was determined not to be cowed, and Judge Steel did allow me to speak up for myself.

When Mr Nutter asked if I hated my stepfather, I said, 'I used to have no feelings about him. I never used to be able to feel hate. But I feel hatred for him today, and that's a good feeling because there is no more fear. I have waited all my life for this, and, please God, jury, you do believe me. But if you don't believe me, that's OK, because I'm here to face him.'

At another point in the cross-examination he accused me of acting and said that being in court was for me 'nearly as good' as being on stage.

Astounded by his comment, I replied firmly, 'The word "good" should not be brought into this. This is not good. This is not good me going home after here, crying my eyes out, having my friends putting themselves out trying to support me, my family coming from Essex and other places and having to drag up the pain of what they remember. That is not good, and I don't know how you can stand there and think it is.'

At another point Mr Nutter questioned, 'This case is about you trying to get away with your lies, is it not?'

My answer was, 'If you can give me one reason why I would put myself through this, one reason. There is no reason for me to be here…Whether he is guilty or innocent in everybody else's eyes, I am going to find it easier when I know I have done everything to put this man where he belongs, so that he doesn't hurt anyone else. I've done my best and now it's down to everyone else to live with their conscience because I can now live with mine.'

Towards the end of his cross-examination of me, Mr Nutter suggested that I had colluded with all the other witnesses to prepare what we were going to say.

I held my head up high and responded, 'And what reason would everybody else have to lie and perjure themselves and stand here in front of a judge and jury and lie? If I am lying, why are they lying?'

'For you,' said the barrister.

'For why? If they know it hasn't happened, why would they lie?'

'For you,' he repeated triumphantly.

'Who would love someone enough, not just one person – maybe you could cajole one person – but a whole group of people? I'm sorry, Mr Nutter, that's just grasping at straws. They're not liars. You will see these people are not liars.'

The cross-examination was finally over and I was permitted to step down. At last, I thought, my part is over. But still I couldn't relax, because I had to watch my friend Donna and my family facing the same kind of interrogation. I felt especially dreadful about putting Donna through the ordeal of the witness box again: Donna hates speaking out in public, and whenever she has to she becomes tongue-tied. But Mr Nutter scored a spectacular home goal when he attacked her for staying with me at the hotel.

He reminded her that witnesses are not supposed to discuss their evidence with each other, and made much of the fact that she was sharing my hotel room. Donna panicked. She froze. She looked like a rabbit caught in the glare of a car's headlights. In the public gallery I was cringing for her, with my hands over my face. Then she turned to the judge and, as if someone had given her a kick up the backside, she launched into a fluent and compelling statement. She said she was there to tell the truth. She told how Mick Garvey used to grab me by the hair and kick me down the street. She said he was always messing with me and that she was the only one I could tell. She even said how hard it was for her to come to court and stand up and talk, but that she was there to tell the truth.

It was impassioned and powerful. I felt so much love for

her. (The truth is, we didn't discuss the case at night: we knew we weren't permitted to, and in any event, we were always too tired, too drained. Although we talked about our childhoods, it was about the fun we had together, belly-flopping over the garden walls at the back of Lark Lane and picking daisies together in Sefton Park.)

There followed a long courtroom discussion about the definition of the word 'messing', which to me and anyone of my age who grew up in the north of England definitely had sexual connotations. When I was little, it was the only word in my vocabulary to express to Donna what Mick Garvey was doing to me, and she certainly understood what I meant, even if I didn't give her details.

It was distressing seeing the other witnesses relive their guilt again: Uncle Gordon was torn apart because he hadn't realised what was going on, and my dad was beside himself because he felt he hadn't done the right thing. Tom gave evidence about our stepfather beating Mum, making us dog-fight each other and the night he had banged on the wall.

I spent the weekend that fell halfway through the trial with Donna, Uncle Gordon and Auntie Anne. I didn't want to go out and socialise because I was emotionally exhausted, but it wasn't easy to sleep. I spent a lot of time on the phone to Courtney and Mick.

The defence didn't call any witnesses, not even character witnesses. I was surprised that Mick Garvey's girlfriend didn't stand up and say what a good partner and father he was, but after that very first day of the first trial I never saw her in the court again. None of his family or his gangster friends appeared in court to say how wonderful he was either.

Next, Mick Garvey himself took the stand, where he implied that I had seduced him by wiggling on his lap. He also told the court I was an accomplished liar from a very early age.

Going into the witness box was the worst thing he could have
done for his own case, and the best for mine. Firstly, the jurors
could see the physical size and menace of him: he made no
effort to appear less threatening. Secondly, he stupidly claimed
he had a perfect memory, and demonstrated this by reciting the
names of all the children on the register in his class at primary
school.

My barrister reeled him in with a simple question: 'Can you
tell me the date you married your first wife?'

He had to admit he couldn't. So much for his brilliant
memory.

It was after his evidence – and questions about his tattoo –
that Judge Steel ordered him to be taken to the cells to have his
genitals photographed. Initially I was mortified, but this
turned to a feeling of satisfaction when I saw the look on Mick
Garvey's face: it was worth it just to make him suffer a bit
more.

When the case resumed, I was recalled to the witness box,
and the photographs were handed to the judge, the jurors and
the lawyers. I hadn't a clue what was on them: nobody had told
me what the tattoo was. I could see a general look of shock on
the faces of the jurors, but I wasn't sure whether this was
simply because they were being confronted with photographs
of male genitalia or because there was something else. My
heart pounded as I waited to hear what would happen next.

After a few moments Mr Nutter stood up and started
questioning me again about the tattoo. 'As you know, it was quite
common public knowledge that Mr Garvey had a tattoo on his
penis...But the mark on Mr Garvey is not a cross.'

I thought, Do you know what? I couldn't care less if it is a
snake with an icepick or a monkey climbing a tree, the fact that
there is a tattoo there proves I saw something. Whatever it is
was probably distorted because my face was so close.

Then the prosecution barrister, Mr Owen, stood up and said, 'You are so eloquent telling Mrs McGovern what isn't there. Would you like to tell her what is?'

Mr Nutter shuffled his papers, and Mr Owen went on, 'As you can see, members of the jury, Mr Garvey has a tattoo of a four-sided star on his penis. To a child of eight in a traumatic situation, all she sees is the shape of a cross.'

When Mr Nutter tried to press his point that it was public knowledge, I said, 'In that case, why didn't I stand up and say he had a tattoo of a four-sided star? If I was told by someone else what it was, surely I would have said that? What I gave you is the image I saw.'

There was a sense of the whole courtroom being in shock at such a dramatic development at this stage in the trial. To me, it was as if God had again given me the tool I needed to survive the ordeal of my life. The cross had come to my aid once more.

After the lawyers' closing speeches and the judge's summing-up, the jury went out to consider their verdicts. This time we didn't have to wait so long, but long enough for me to be reduced to a state of nervous exhaustion. Back they came into court, and the foreman stood up. The charges were read out and he spoke the words I had been longing to hear: 'Guilty. Guilty. Guilty. Guilty.'

As each one was spoken, my heart soared. It was a combination of relief and joy, and a wonderful feeling that I had taken back control. Finally, after all those years of Mick Garvey telling me that nobody would believe me, here was a public statement that people did in fact believe me. And I had those 'guiltys' to prove it. I felt emotionally wrung out, but we were all exultant: we'd got what we'd come for. He was found guilty of raping me on three occasions and of indecently assaulting me. Ten further charges of rape and indecent assault were to remain on file.

Judge Steel said that there was no need to wait for reports on him before sentence, and that he would have no room for appeal. She was very abrupt with him, telling him that he had scarred me for life and that what he had done was evil. She sentenced him to thirteen years the counts of rape, which were to run concurrently with five years for the indecent assault. He was ordered to sign the sex offenders' register for life.

Thirteen years, I thought. It was one year for every year of my life he had taken.

There was a clear partition separating the dock from the rest of the court. Mick Garvey turned and looked at me, and there were tears running down his face. This time, he didn't draw his hand across his throat. There were no threats. I was shivering and shaking, and Donna, Tom and Gordon were all holding on to me, telling me it was OK. As he passed through the doorway out of the court, we heard a long, guttural howl, like a wounded animal.

When I heard that blood-curdling noise, all elation drained from me and I collapsed in tears. I felt guilty that I could have caused so much pain to another human being. I didn't care that it was him, the man who had caused *me* so much suffering. All I could think was that it was a person, with feelings, and I was responsible. At that moment my emotions were mixed: I was happy for myself and yet guilty for what I had done to a fellow human being.

Early in my life I swore to God that if He saw me safe through life so that I could be a good woman and a good mother, I would never knowingly harm another living soul. I swore I would never intentionally hurt anyone, and yet here I was, taking the last years of someone's life. I didn't feel jubilant for long: guilt set in the minute I heard that howl.

When I had first heard the guilty verdicts, my main

emotion had been relief: now everyone would know that I had told the truth – I wasn't the liar he made me out to be as a child, and again tried to brand me as in court. I'd have been devastated if he'd got off, but I couldn't rejoice at what had happened to him, even though it was his own actions that had put him there.

The first thing I did when we walked out of the courtroom was to ring Mick and my sons, David and Gordon. Naturally, they had been following the case closely, with bulletins from me every evening. Now I could tell them of our victory.

As I finished my phone calls, Mr Owen approached me.

'You've done all my work for me,' he said, shaking my hand. 'I feel as if I'm being paid for nothing.'

I told him that it was thanks to him that I had the strength to face the court every day, and I gave him a thank-you card that I had written the previous evening at the hotel. He asked me to do him a favour by letting him have a copy of my poem 'Mental/Physical' for his wife, because she worked with children with problems.

Then I stood outside the court and as every member of the jury came out, I handed them each a thank-you card. I would have given them out even if the verdict had gone against me: I felt they deserved my thanks for sitting there for nine days, listening to the story of my life. On the cards I had written: 'Thank you for being so understanding. I am so sorry for what you have had to endure, and I thank you for coming to the right decision.'

I gave a card to the Crown Prosecution Service solicitor, Lionel Copes, who had been such a tremendous support to me all the way through, and I tried to leave one for Judge Steel, but was told a judge can't accept anything from anyone involved in a case.

I saw John Garvey that day, Mick's younger brother. He was

in court for the sentencing. He shook my hand, and said, 'Well done, girl.'

I held his hand and said gently, 'I'm sorry, John.'

I didn't feel it was a joyous occasion for him. His brother, whom he had relied on all his life, had gone to prison for a long time. I owe a lot to John: he was the catalyst; he opened the book and set everything in motion. I felt sorry for him, and also very indebted.

As it was by now late afternoon, we all spilled into a little pub near the courts to have a celebratory drink. It was too crowded and I began to feel trapped and claustrophobic among strangers, so Uncle Gordon took us to another bar he knew, where there was a dance floor and a karaoke machine.

I have a terrible singing voice, but obviously the importance of the occasion overcame my inhibitions and I took the microphone. 'Before I sing this,' I said, looking out at my friends and family, 'I want to thank you all for being so supportive and seeing me through this. I'm finally at the end of this chapter of my life, and it is thanks to you that I have survived this far. What happened to me will never be forgotten, but I've finally done the right thing, and I want to thank you all for being here for me.'

We were all a bit tearful, and exhausted, and when Donna and I got back to the hotel room, we hugged and, for the first time in nine days, slept like lambs.

Epilogue

Closure. I heard the word 'closure' many times in my battle to bring Mick Garvey to justice, and afterwards it seemed to be on countless people's lips: 'Now you have closure.' But of course I didn't. It's too easy, too glib, to think that because my abuser was behind bars, all the evils of my childhood would be wiped out. There is no such thing as closure – there is never an end. I will take my abuse to the grave with me; it's with me every day; it's what has made me who I am. I have had to fight all my life to make sure that it doesn't take over, but I can never deny that it happened, or that it affected me.

I had been told about closure so often that I really expected there to be a magical shift inside me from the day my abuser was sentenced, but nothing dramatic happened, and this is something I wish I'd been prepared for, and something I hope that others who read my book, and who have been abused themselves, will understand. Yes, justice helps – justice is your right and you should seek it. You will feel cleansed when the truth is in the open, but don't be fooled into thinking you will be a different person afterwards. You will still have to live with what you have always lived with.

I did, in some ways, feel different. I remember thinking, I have been a child all my life, but as a child I was forced to be a woman. The child is still within me, but now the trial is over, and what she said has been accepted and believed, she has grown up. The child and the woman have finally met and are now one.

So the trial did help. But my life has been a constant healing process, and this will go on until the day I die. I am still, and always will be, ambushed by flashbacks. I was recently watching an episode of *Coronation Street* in which one of the characters told his son to 'get upstairs' (for entirely innocent reasons) and it took me straight back to Knapp Road and Mick Garvey ordering me to tidy my room. The flashback was so intense that I started crying. But late that night, when everyone else was asleep, I deliberately went through the memory in my head, dealing with my own feelings about it. Slowly, bit by bit, I am emptying all the boxes where I have shut away the things from my past that I couldn't face at the time.

I am still frightened of creaking floorboards and turning door handles, I still have feelings of inadequacy and self-disgust, and at times I still lack confidence and self-esteem. At these times, I remind myself I have a great deal to be proud of, because unlike so many people who are abused, I never turned to drugs, alcohol, self-harm or prostitution, and although I have had problems with my mental health, I have dealt with them and kept myself sane.

After the immediate euphoria of the trial had passed, my life felt very flat. Ever since Mick Garvey had walked into my life when I was four, which was nearly forty years earlier, I had wanted to put him behind bars. At the back of my mind, throughout everything that happened to me, I had felt sure that one day I would see him face the consequences of his actions. I had spent the past two years preparing myself for the battle, studying the law, thinking about my evidence and being utterly preoccupied by the case.

When it was all over, I knew I should have been delighted to settle back into a cosy, happy family life, but I felt lost. I didn't know where to go or what to do. I no longer had my fight, my drive, my reason to get up in the morning.

Consequently, I found my own way of coping, not one that I am proud of. One day a couple of months after my stepfather went to prison, I was meeting a friend in a nearby town but was early. It was raining and I saw an amusement arcade with a sign that read, 'Tea and coffee free'. I thought, I'll treat myself to ten quid on the games machines and have a cup of coffee. I'd never seriously gambled before, but I had played arcade games for a bit of fun when we'd been on holiday. By the time I was due to meet my friend I had won £60. It's the classic way that gamblers get hooked: an early win and the feeling that it will always be like that.

For me, it was also oblivion. I soon returned. While I was in the arcade, everything else was forgotten. All I could concentrate on were the flashing lights, the soothing *ching, ching, ching* of the machines. It was hypnotic, and it made me feel secure. For over a year the arcade became my haven. I went every day. I had a few wins, but most of the time I was chasing my losses. Then one day I came to my senses. I was in the toilet at the arcade when I looked at a poster I had seen many times before, but for some reason I felt compelled to read it properly. It was for Gamblers Anonymous, and it offered help to anyone who felt their gambling was out of control. I went to a meeting – only one, but that was all I needed. It made me realise that gambling was a way of running away. I wasn't confronting my problems; I was hiding from them.

I took a close look at myself and I realised that gambling was filling a hole in my life. I had to find other, better things to do with my time and energy. Throughout all this, none of my family had realised what was happening. I had used some money that Mick and I had been putting away for holidays and emergencies, but I carefully scrimped and saved until I had replaced it all. Only then did I confess to him. He was very understanding. Having been through his own problems, he wasn't going to criticise me for mine, and he could see that I had been strong enough to sort it out.

Now and again I still get the urge to go into an arcade and play the machines, and once or twice I have succumbed, but I have been sensible enough to walk away soon afterwards and now I just have the odd flutter, usually on holiday. I know that gambling is a destroyer of lives, and if I had my way, all arcades would be shut down except in holiday resorts.

Perhaps one of the reasons there was such a void in my life after the trial is because, once again, I'd slipped through the net. In my childhood I'd been without support, and here I was again on my own. After a trial like the one I had been through, the Probation Service and Victim Support should have liaised with me to inform me about the services that were available to me, but nobody contacted me and I was left to get on with things as best I could. I think this was partly because the case was heard in Liverpool and I lived in Essex, but once again authority seemed to have turned its back on me.

It was not until three years later that the Probation Service got in touch, and I now have a great victim liaison officer, Marian Levy. I have survived all these years without counselling, but it is good to know that Marian is there when I need her. She asked me if I would agree to be filmed reading my poem 'Mental/Physical', which I did. At my suggestion, the film editor cut pictures of me as a small child in with film of me as an adult reading the words. The tape was shown at a conference for Essex Probation Service, and I was told later that people cried when they saw it. Probation officers are used to working with the perpetrators, so I think it was good for them to see it from the other perspective.

I try never to use the word 'victim' to refer to my situation. 'Victim' would hand the victory to my abuser. The word I use is 'survivor', because that's what I am. Mick Garvey saw me as his victim; he didn't count on me being a survivor.

After another few months of drifting aimlessly, I decided to take stock of my life. Mick Garvey was in prison, my brothers and my two sons were all settled, and even my baby Courtney was now a teenager. It was time to work out what I wanted to do with the rest of my life.

I'd developed a taste for education when I'd taken my GCSEs fifteen years earlier, in Liverpool, but I'd never had the chance to go any further: now, I felt, was the time to start my brain working again. I decided to train as a counsellor, and I found a suitable course at my local adult education centre. There are three components to the course: counselling skills, counselling theory and psychology. Each takes fifteen weeks of part-time study. When I signed up, I announced that I wanted to do the first two parts at the same time. I felt I had lost so much time in my life that I needed to cram in as much as possible. My tutor said I could try, but she warned me that I might find it far too intense, and that although several people had tried doing two at once, no one had succeeded for over eight years. Undeterred, I got stuck in. It was hard, but I was determined, and guess what? I made it. Once I have completed the third part of the course, I am hoping to counsel others.

I feel I can be particularly valuable to anyone who is facing a court case against someone who has abused them. Nobody told me how difficult it would be in court, how the flashbacks would come, how the defence barrister would try to diminish me, how my emotions would be stirred up. The man in the dock has a legal team at his disposal all the way through, and he knows what to expect. The victims get far less help, and it rarely comes from anyone who has experienced anything similar. I would like to share what I know with others who have yet to get there.

To convict a paedophile, the witnesses have to be strong enough to survive the barrage of questions they receive from the defence. I can give advice on court procedures and how to appear in court. Even when a victim is telling the truth, the pain of reliving the experience may mean that their body language is negative, which makes them look as if they are lying. Remember, children who have been abused have been taught to feel guilty from an early age, and that sense of guilt may compromise their ability to deliver evidence strongly.

I now give lectures as a volunteer to the Probation Service, mental health workers, women's groups and counsellors, anyone who I think may need help understanding what it is like to be abused from a very early age. When you have lived with shame for so long, it's hard to break your silence, and the last thing any abuse victim needs is an unsympathetic ear.

All my life I have enjoyed helping others, and early on I promised myself that my own traumas wouldn't affect my ability to give to others. Now I believe my experience of those terrible events of my childhood can actually be put to good use.

As well as my counselling course and lectures, I am heavily involved in the fundraising for Courtney's football team. She's a talented player who loves the game, and I do everything I can to support her. She's also doing very well at school, and I'm hoping she'll take advantage of all the educational opportunities that were denied to me.

As for the rest of my wonderful family, they are all doing well. My two sons and both my brothers live near me, and we are very close. There's nothing I enjoy more than having them all, with their partners and children, around me, eating food that I have cooked.

As for Mick Garvey, I'm delighted that he is in Walton Jail, where I hope he is having a tough time adjusting to his new status of paedophile. As a criminal, he never quite made the grade in the gangster ranks, but now he'll find himself among the lowest of the low, where he belongs.

My biggest hope is that readers of this book who have been abused will draw from my story the courage to come forward and to pursue justice. I'm not pretending it's an easy road, but it is a very rewarding one.

I think about my stepfather occasionally: when I gaze up at a lovely clear sky, when I see flowers bobbing in the breeze, when I walk to the shops for a paper, when I make a sandwich and a cup of tea, when I go for a drink. These are things he can no longer do.

I know he goes to bed at night with hatred for me in his heart, and I'm glad. He now knows what it feels like. I hope I am haunting him. He will be seventy when he is first eligible for parole, and I'll be there fighting his application. I accept, however, that one day he will walk free, and I expect that he will come looking for me.

I won't hide.

I was afraid. I am afraid no more.

'CRY OF A CHILD'

Look at my picture, see how innocent I look.
That was the week my virginity was took.
I could not understand it. I was only three feet ten.
He laughed as I cried, then he raped me again.
Did anyone hear me as I screamed out loud?
'Shut up, bitch,' he said. 'You're mine, it's allowed.'
No one to save me, alone again. I grieved.
Who should I tell? Who would have believed?
In silence I suffered as my knickers he tore.
I became a slave to his lust, his own child whore,
A toy for his perversion, a nonentity for his play;
His paedophile intentions lived with me every day.
So I found a secret part of me where I could go and hide.
As the terror began, my fear he was denied.
I lay like a stone. I was only five, you see.
I found my thoughts wandering to the time I would be free.
I swore if I survived to be a woman and a wife
My day in court would come, to describe my painful life.
No melodramatics, no tears, fear or hate,
I'll stare into his eyes and chuck in the bait.
His denials and swearing, his lies and defence
Came to the ears of those sitting on the fence,
Disgust in the jury's eyes, self-hatred in me.
As the case unfolded, I felt myself pull free.
I was unleashed in public, my most important day,
He thought he'd left his past behind, thought I'd gone away.
He forgot me, you see, this man who marred my mind.
I stood like a stone, so cold yet so kind,
For still I felt pity, not for me but him,
I was still a loving person, in spite of his sin.